Play Ball!

by Bruce Blackwell

PEARSON

Glenview, Illinois • Boston, Massachusetts • Chandler, Arizona
Upper Saddle River, New Jersey

Let's play ball!
What to do?
Ask friends to play with you.

friends

ACKNOWLEDGEMENTS

I would like to acknowledge the assistance of all the people who read the manuscript before the book was released. The list is too long to name, but I would like to everyone who played a role in making this book possible, especially Dr. Paulette Millord and Samara Gracia. I would also like to thank my mother for bringing me into this world, and my father for always supporting my writing. I especially would like to give a big thanks, hugs and kisses to my two wonderful princesses, my lovely daughters, Rishanna and Richlyn.

INTRODUCTION

Is it ever a good time to take revenge against the system, or the actors paid by the system? Is it normal to be vengeful after a person is wronged by society or another person?

These are questions I struggled with while writing this book. For some odd reason, I kept trying to find justification for the actions taken by the characters I created for this story. I don't feel guilty or anything like that, but I don't want the readers walking away unsatisfied after reading my book. After all, it's just a story, right? Is it? Maybe it's art imitating life? Maybe it's too much of a reality for black people? It very well could be, but I know better, so I'd go as far as to say matter-of-factly, it is. I didn't write this book to give black people reasons to reconsider the approach taken when a loved one is murdered. I wrote this book to open the eyes of the black community to an ongoing struggle that we have had to face in this country forever, because we have been forced into a position of fear, and keep wondering what would happen if we ever let go of that fear. I also wrote this book to hopefully give black folks a better outlook on the strength of family, black unity, our history as a stolen people, and the interconnection that we all have with each other, through our ancestors who were illegally kidnapped from AFRICA and became disoriented and disconnected in the WEST through slavery.

How can we honestly call this book a figment of my creative imagination when so many black families have lived the reality of the horror of this story almost daily? There are so many black victims of police murder in the world; it would take an additional chapter to list all of the names of the victims in this book to honor them. My very important questions for black people are: how can we hold back the zeal for vengeance for the unjust murder of 12-year-old Tamir Rice at the hands of police officer, Timothy Loehmann? How can we allow George Zimmerman to continue to roam the streets freely after he unjustly disregarded the existence and livelihood of Trayvon Martin? You see, it doesn't take a creative genius to write a book centered around the unjust killings of black children and black people in America, because America, as a nation, was built on the injustices it created for black people, from the time the former despicable thugs from America via way of England, illegally kidnapped our ancestors on the continent, to the time they brought them to the west to be illegally enslaved.

There's always a story to tell, but the multitude of lives ruined, stolen, and taken through slavery, makes it an endless process for all the wordsmiths out there who have the ability to cipher or port-manteau words into educational, entertaining and, heartfelt stories. This book is my dedication to the great awakening of not just black people, but the entire world, to the malfeasance of white suprema-cy against humanity.

When will it ever be okay for us to take revenge against white supremacy?

CANDACE'S STORY

My dad told me that I was his pride and joy when I was born. However, he and my mother thought they were going to have a boy until the ultrasound revealed otherwise. No fret though, because my dad preferred a girl anyway. My mother only wanted a healthy child, regardless of what the sex was. My father decided to name me Candace because he said I was royalty and would grow up to be somebody's queen one day since he had planned to raise me as his princess. He told me that he learned the origin of the name while browsing through a book of African names that a friend had suggested. My dad was always going to the library to research everything, so he became pretty well-known to the staff at the Brooklyn library. There was always a quest to quench his thirst for knowledge and to learn something new. My dad spent most of his free time at the library for reasons most people wouldn't be able to figure out, but we surmised it was mostly to exercise his mind and to keep it well-tuned. It's not as if my dad was anti-social or anything like that, but he enjoyed spending his free time construc- tively. When he decided to go back to school, the library became his second home. My mother found him to be very different from the other men she dated in her past, because he didn't really waste his precious time doing what most other men his age were doing; such as skirts chasing, being out partying all the time, and wasting money and energy on frivolous bullshit. Everything that my dad did, served a purpose in his life. Besides, my father didn't have the financial means to partake in too many leisure activities anyway.

Getting back to my name...it didn't take too much convincing on the part of my dad to get my mom to agree to the name Candace. Once my dad explained what the name meant, my mom was all for it. Since she was his big queen, it was the normal order for him to name me his little queen, since he didn't get to name his wife. I love my name. Candace is actually a royal name, deriving from the term Kandake, a title for a queen from the ancient African Kingdom of Kush. It also means pure and innocent. I guess in my daddy's eyes when I was born, I was his pure and innocent princess who would one day become somebody's queen. I'm happy he named me that, because the name is befitting. I feel like a Candace. I don't know if any other name would've suited me so perfectly. Whenever my par- ents told me stories about the joy that my birth brought to them, it filled me with pride and joy. Unfortunately, I find it unusually ab- normal nowadays too few black parents take the time to instill pride in their children like my parents instilled in me. Too many black people trust the school system to completely educate their children, without reinforcing and instilling pride at home, by teaching them their true history. The white school systems in America have convinced everyone that black life started with slavery, and it's sad that even more black scholars and academics have regurgitated that false narrative. Education should always start at home anyway. Too many of our people just expect ancestral pride in their children's lives to just develop miraculously on its own. It takes a lot of work and I'm grateful that I have parents who reinforced it in me on a daily basis. I appreciate my parents for educating me at home, but I'm especially thankful for having grown up with a father who understood the importance of home education. The blanket shaming of black people by the media and white society as a whole, always begins with the conflagration that we are all descendants of slaves, as opposed to white people being murderers, thieves, rapists, kidnappers, and extortionists who enslaved African doctors, lawyers, scholars and so on. These white enslavers were not taking their time to learn the credentials of the people they captured. Every black person stolen from Africa was subjected to inhumane treatment because of white greed and racism. My dad's experience as a black man before moving to America was very different than most black men in this country. As an immigrant to this country, my dad realized not too long after he arrived to the United States, the failure of the school system in urban America, or Brooklyn, New York, where he specifically lived. He made it his job to teach me things beyond the realm of their curriculum that the school system purposely failed to teach about black history. My dad had never heard of Black History Month, because where he came from Black History is celebrated year round. The school system here purposely tries to separate black people from their history by using subgroups and subcultures as part of their division. My dad is very proud of his homeland of Haiti. He constantly reminds me that Haitian history is part of black history because America wouldn't be what it is today without the assistance of Haitian people. We are all inclusive.

While my teachers at school were busy quoting Dr. King's "I Have a Dream" speech, my dad was teaching me about Jean-Jacques Dessalines decapitating the heads of his former enslavers and slaughtering them, during the Haitian Revolution. Dessalines even took the lives of some his own black people who refused to revolt against slavery, because he saw them as a hindrance and danger to the liberation of the Haitian people. There was no room for error, and anybody who didn't want to fight for his or her freedom was viewed as a traitor and possible informer or sellout to the movement. Emperor Jean Jacques Dessalines saw the Haitian Revolution as freedom beyond the borders of Haiti. He envisioned a free black republic for all black people, and all black people all over the world were welcomed into his kingdom. My dad was also fascinated with Malcolm X after reading the book, The Autobiography of Malcolm X, so he also taught me about the defiant stance that Malcolm X took against the marginalization and subjugation of black people in this country. My dad, to this day, still loves the philosophy of Malcolm X, as well as his redemption as a man. He also taught me the history of other black revolutionaries like Denmark Vesey, Nat Turner, Harriet Tubman, Bessie Coleman, Stokely Carmicheal, Marcus Garvey, and many others in America, and even more African revolutionaries in Africa like Steve Biko, Patrice Lumumba, Kwame Nkrumah and Thomas Sankara, to name a few, who fought and helped black people stand up to their oppressors around the world. My father made it clear to me that not all black leaders of the past have been passive and submissive, and very few of them preached any type of nonviolence that would force compliance to their own marginalization. "Freedom is not free, and bloodshed is an accepted reality of any real revolution," he would tell me. "Whenever a group of people have to peacefully beg for their freedom from their oppressor, keep in mind that handed freedom would come with certain restrictions, conditions, and guidelines that would still benefit and offer privileges to the oppressor, for allowing such freedom," my dad reminded me. My dad was not a proponent of any type of passive movements on the part of black people, in order to completely liberate ourselves. Not that he was anti-Dr. King, or his philosophy, but he wished that Dr. King had further researched Mahatma Gandhi, before adopting Gandhi's nonviolent philosophy and approach for his own Civil Rights movement in America. My father made me research Gandhi, so I could see for myself that Gandhi was a pedophile and racist who referred to Africans in South Africa as Kaffir, another term for nigger that was used in by racist people there. "There's no reason why this racist piece of shit should be put on a pedestal by anybody around the world," my father said. That propelled me to look further into Gandhi's work in South Africa, and the reasons he was able to sell himself to the world as a man of peace and a revolutionary at the same time. I'm thankful that I grew up with a resourceful father who provided me with the right tools to assess most of the situations that I'm faced with in this world to this day. Not every child is so lucky. Everything my dad has ever told me has always been proven to be true, so it's difficult not to hold him in the highest regard. Gandhi was in fact a narcissistic pedophile, and racist, who thought of Africans as being less intelligent than everybody else in the world. I still question why a picture of Gandhi is hanging at the Dr. Martin Luther King Center. Did the people responsible for the center even bother to do their research on Gandhi?

My upbringing was fun, stimulating, intellectual, exciting, and educational because my father made it that way in every aspect. He especially tried to make learning fun, because he understood it was the passage to intellectual, psychological, mental and emotional freedom. As a result, I developed a voracious appetite for learning and reading. Though my mother was also very intelligent and capable, she allocated the duties of my intellectual development to my father. She trusted my father's intellect, decision-making ability, morals, principles and his leadership to mold me in the best possible way to become a productive member of society. My mother's primary concern was to provide a stable, clean, and safe environment where learning was conducive for me and peaceful for her and my dad. Though my father was the primary breadwinner, he and my mom worked as a unit to make sure I had a secure and better financial future than they did as children. My father didn't place too much emphasis on material possessions, but he definitely believed in establishing generational wealth for his family. To him, purchasing a family home was the best source of generational wealth, and he dedicated himself to becoming a homeowner after I was born. Other than that, he worked simply because he had responsibilities to my mother and me, but his spare time was spent learning and absorbing as much knowledge as he could. If my father had his way, he would be lecturing daily at all the universities, to open the minds of black people walking around with mistaken identities they've adopted, or forced upon them, all over the world. According to my dad, all of our identities as black people in the West are mistaken. He would say, "These people docked their ships in different parts of the New World, and our ancestors were beaten and forced to adopt their last names, religion, language, culture, and their bullshit customs, which created, not just a false sense of identity, but also a mistaken identity, for all the African people in the Diaspora.

Whether our ancestors were enslaved in America, the Caribbean, Central America, or South America, we are all living with a mistaken identity and a false sense of who we are, because most of us can't trace our ancestry back to Africa to our specific tribes. Our research into our roots and heritage, unfortunately, usually ends with the last name of the enslavers who kidnapped our forefathers. We now call ourselves American, Brazilian, Haitian, Jamaican, Costa Rican, and so on, because those nationalities were forced upon our ancestors. We can't even communicate with one another, because they also took away our native tongues, which connected our ancestors."

My dad has always been keen on the psychological effects of slavery and how it has forced upon black people identities we still can't even relate to today, and cultural norms we've had to adhere to, that are completely against our nature as African people. My family is not a typical Haitian-American family. I say Haitian-American, only because I was born and raised in America. However, my parents are one hundred percent Haitian born, raised with Haitian customs, principles, and morals, and they are very proud of it, and have passed those customs and principles on to me. Though my dad has never been ashamed of his background and heritage, and always made sure that I understood that shame was something that insecure and inferior people use to project their emotional instabilities and discomforts onto other people, he questioned the validity of his nationality, because at the very core, he understands

8

that he's an African. "No matter what part of the world you live in, people will always see you first as an African, and you should never be ashamed of that," he would tell me. "The different labels and nationalities that we have allowed the colonizers to bestow upon us, in order to stigmatize us, have also created separation among us as African people," he reinforced all the time. I learned from my father that we can't be so attached to nationalities forced upon us, that we forget the fact that we were all once related and came from the same region in Africa. Most enslaved black people all over the world came from West Africa originally, and we must never forget that. My dad never fails to emphasize that racism and white supremacy are built on white people's shameful history, their own inferiority and inse-curities, as it relates to the strength of black people and their frailties in a world that is dominated by black culture in every aspect.

I learned very early in life that I was going to have to prove that I'm twice as smart as everybody else, just because I was born black, female and daughter of immigrants in America. My dad talked to me about all the obstacles that I would face while growing up. He was always transparent and held no punches when it came to im-parting knowledge and bringing awareness to my adversities. My dad gave me a great educational head start and springboard very early in my life. This world is lucky to have me because my daddy told me so.

KANE'S STORY

I have no idea whether my conception was special to my parents or not, but I know they had me right out of high school. My mom and dad were high school sweethearts at Madison Park Technical Vocational high school in Boston, but more specifically, the Roxbury section of Boston, the black part of Boston, before gentrification changed the demographics. I was conceived on prom night. You know most fathers and their glorified stories, right? Well, my dad is no different. My dad swore he was the man when he was in high school, and my mom was just the cheerleader who couldn't resist the big husky football hunk that he was. That's my dad's version of his stories, always filled with glorifications, even when it's unnecessary. My mom always had a different version of the story to tell. According to her, my dad spent weeks begging her to go out on a date with him. Even though she was a cheerleader, she didn't want to date a football player, or any athlete for that matter. She finally agreed to go to the movies with him, because he was a gentleman and kept writing her poetry daily. "The art of courting a woman is long gone. Your dad used to buy me flowers regularly, and would infringe on other people's poetry by plagiarizing and tried to pass them as his own, just to impress me. Nowadays, men just ask women if they wanna fuck right up front, and think that's the right way to court them, and so many women accept that bullshit. I'm not raising you to address women that way. You better learn how to treat a lady from your father. I'll make sure he teach you everything he knows." Mom said during one of our conversations. My mother could be blunt at times, and I love her for it. My mom thought a lot of my dad's original poetry was corny, but she appreciated his effort and sweetness, nonetheless. My dad was definitely no Shakespeare, but he would steal a line or two from some of the most popular rappers of his time and made it sound good enough to call it poetry. LL Cool J was one of my dad's favorite rappers, and the only rapper at the time who didn't mind showing his vulnerabilities to the ladies. My dad definitely stole a few lines from him and MC Shan as well, and my mom knew that. After a while, my mom was smitten by him, and in no time they became a couple. They were both seniors when they started dating. My dad knew the only way he was gonna go to college, was if he was offered a full scholarship for football. He was the star linebacker on the team, but he wasn't really into school like that. Education was secondary to him, and he definitely was not a five-star recruit. My dad saw football as an escape and his ticket off the streets, with the possibility of a better life, which were the primary reasons why he played the game. However, he also saw nothing wrong with a backup plan in case football didn't work out. My dad was all about securing his future. He wanted to get his paper in order very early in life. Struggle was not an option for my pop. Since his high school was a vocational school, he took advantage of the vocational trades that they offered at Madison Park Technical Vocational high school. He spent a lot of extra time learning everything that he could about plumbing. The plumbing teacher sometimes had to kick my dad out of his classroom, because he never wanted to leave. He wanted to graduate high school as a licensed plumber, and he ended up doing just that. It was a good thing that my dad thought of a backup plan, because during his fifth game against Hyde Park high school in his senior season, he tore his ACL. The scouts stopped coming to watch his games, and the offers from the colleges never came. This was the final moment when my dad realized he was expendable and dispensable when it came to football. My father was fine with that. He knew upon graduation he was going to be a certified and licensed plumber and the jobs were plentiful in Boston.

Meanwhile, my mom took advantage of the cosmetology and hairdressing program offered at the high school. She wanted to be a licensed cosmetologist and hairdresser upon graduation. She would braid my father's hair into cornrows and sometimes did her girlfriends' hair at the house for practice, until she got so good at it, she didn't even have time to herself, because her talent and skills were on high demand. By the time my mother graduated from high school, she was a licensed cosmetologist and hairdresser with a long list of clients. My parents became inseparable during their senior year in high school. My mom was the brown skin, pretty and petite cheerleader with the perfect body, and my dad was the dark skinned stud, but shy linebacker on the football team. Both of my parents were outgoing, but they didn't hang out with the popular crowd in high school. Away from football and cheerleading, they spent most of their time together. Both of my parents were driven people who wanted more in life than the average Joe, but college was not the gateway to their dreams. My mom never even thought about college. She wanted to do what she enjoyed most, which was hair. That's all she ever talked about since she was a kid, according to my grandmother. My mom's dream of becoming a hairdresser, and eventually a business owner, would not be denied.

To this day, it is still unknown whether my dad was a virgin or not, when he started dating my mom, but he also didn't seem all that experienced either, according to my mom. I did say my mom was blunt and too transparent at times, didn't I? My dad might've boasted that he had been with a few women, but according to his actions, he was more of a neophyte at best on prom night, at which time they decided to finally consummate their relationship. My dad had no idea what he was doing, and neither did my mom, based on her best recollection and the most honest way of telling me the story. I have always been cool with my parents because they were young when I was born, and we've talked about almost everything and anything ever since I graduated from high school. My mom had told me once that my dad was only humping between her tightly closed legs because she was afraid to go all the way. While my dad was putting all his effort into those tightly closed thighs, he imagined it was the best vagina he had ever tasted, until my mom asked in a shy and scared voice, "Is it in yet?" My dad was going HAM! It was at that point that my mom knew that my dad was a virgin just like her. It was the blind leading the blind. My dad was humping the hell out of her inner thighs. Eventually, he would be led to the right place, with her guidance, and it didn't take long for my dad to let out his seed, without as much as fully breaking my mother's hymen the first time they had sex. It was that quick. To this day, my mother still thinks she was a virgin after I was conceived. My father really thought he took her virginity that night, but that's not what my mother recalled. After a while, sex became a normal/regular thing between them, but my mom had discovered four weeks after the prom, and a couple of weeks before graduation, that she was pregnant with me. That was not in the plans.

After my dad's football injury, he knew his chances of ever playing football at the university level were slim to none, because he needed almost a year to recuperate from his ACL tear. It's not as if my dad was a 5-star recruit that schools were willing to wait on him to heal. Sitting out for a year, wishing upon a star was not his style, and he had a baby on the way to care and provide for, so he decided to focus on becoming a full time plumber. My dad also decided to propose to my mom, and they got married a month before I was born. Having a bastard child was not an option for either of my parents. They both strongly believed in the family unit, and they both decided they wanted to get married to each other. My dad came from a two-parent home and they always emphasized the importance of marriage and the family unit. My parents decided to name me Kane, because my mother's favorite rapper at the time was Big Daddy Kane and she really liked the name, and since my dad liked him, too, they didn't have a problem with the name Kane. I learned my name had nothing to do with the bible from them. For two years, I was my parents' pride and joy, until my little brother, Jeff, came along, and then my sister, Cynthia, came a couple of years later after the birth of Jeff. My parents made it work as best as they could. We never felt like we were poor, or lacked for anything because my parents made sure we never went without. I'm almost certain there were struggles along the way in the beginning of their marriage that I'm sure we were not privy to as children, but my parents did a great job shielding us from the difficulties and struggles they faced as young parents and a married couple earlier in our lives. Eventually they would purchase a home when I was around seven years old, and life would get a little easier for everyone in the family.

Of course, as an adult I learned that there's no such thing as a perfect relationship, but I'll be damned if I didn't think my family was the perfect family. I still do to this day, thanks to my dad, because he has always held his position as the man of the house, and my mom has never gotten in his way. I thank both of them for giving me and my siblings the best possible life experiences they could offer. We are always there for one another. We are a very close-knit family. That's exactly how I hope my own family to be one day.

KANE'S FAMILY

It didn't take long after my wife and I got married for her to decide she wanted to become a mother. We barely spent two years alone in the 2500 sq ft, four-bedroom, two-and-a-half-bath home that we purchased, after my wife, Candace, started having baby fever. My wife did her due diligence to make sure our child was going to be raised in a loving environment, and a place where education was prioritized.

I grew up in a family where my father instilled certain values in me that most men my age lacked, while I was in the military. I was reared in the most traditional way possible. My dad was the provider and head of household, and my mother stayed home to take care of me and my two siblings until we were of school age. To establish her own financial independence, my mom initially worked part-time at this hair salon whenever she could, just so she could have her own little stash. Though everything wasn't always copacetic all the time, the family managed to get along well. We were never exposed to any quarrels that my parents may have had. As children, we were never involved in grown folks' business. We stayed in our place and our parents made sure of it. We hardly knew when my parents had any disagreements because my parents made it their business to always show love and solidarity in our presence, all of the time. They were always a united front, especially when it came to disciplining us. I never once heard my father cussed or raised his voice at my mother, nor she at him. Never! After my parents got married a few months after graduating from high school, the responsibilities as adults came quicker than they could've ever anticipated. My father knew he had to step up as a man, because he was raised with the values and principles that a man is responsible to take care of his family, no matter what. My father also had Southern roots, so he understood family responsibility. My paternal grandparents were from the South. For some reason, a lot of black southern families tend to have more cohesiveness and principles that they follow that usually keep the family strong and together.

While working at his full-time job, my dad took on extra hours to save enough money for an apartment before my mother gave birth to me. She also managed to save some of her money to buy some of the things she thought she would need once I arrived. My dad didn't want my mother anywhere near perms or any type of chemical that would affect the birth of their child, so my mom only braided people's hair while she was pregnant. My dad had heard about the correlation between the chemical used in hair perms and cancer, so he was adamant that my mother did not expose herself or her baby to any perm at anybody's salon. It was a time when men were also braiding their hair in cornrows, so my mom had plenty of clients from her community, thanks to NBA star Allen Iverson making wearing cornrows trendy among the youth. Indefinitely working for a local company as a plumber was not part of my dad's long-term plans, though. My dad was looking ahead, and he wanted to establish his own plumbing company in the near future. First, he had to master the trade. His own plumbing business would come soon enough.

Meanwhile, my mom used her hairdresser skills to earn money braiding people's hair in her kitchen when she was pregnant, as well as the local hair salon, after she gave birth to me, whenever they were short-staffed, and when she was available to work. She took on more clients after my siblings and I started attending school. Back then, vocational schools like Madison Park Technical Vocational high school were imperative to the growth of the black middle class. These schools offered students the opportunity to learn bodywork, plumbing, and a long list of other trades they could put to use right out of high school to earn a living. Once the racist system noticed the progress and opportunities these programs offered to a lot of black families who elevated themselves to the middle class, they decided to eliminate these programs from the inner city high schools, and then all these private for-profit trade schools started sprouting everywhere. Now, black folks have to bury themselves in student loan debt, in order to learn a trade. The destruction of the black middle class was well orchestrated, according to my dad who had managed to reap the benefits of learning a trade for free in high school. My dad may not have gone to college, but he was an avid reader, and kept up with the latest news. He had a regular subscription to the Wall Street Journal, the Boston Globe, and the New York Times. As a child, I was forced to read these newspapers to stay informed. My dad would always say that knowledge is always hidden between the pages of a book, magazine, or newspaper. It's cheap, so you might as well gain it. My dad was a wealth of knowledge, but his intelligence was often overlooked, because he was wearing dirty overalls most of the time, due to the nature of his work. People's prejudices and stereotypes led to them underestimating his intelligence a lot of the time. Please don't even get him started on talking about plumbing. My dad mastered his craft in no time. He always told us to do everything to our best ability and with the most pride, no matter what the job is. He taught us so much as children, but more importantly, he was a highly moral and principled man.

My father would tell us how the reconstruction period brought tremendous growth to industrial America, which helped build the white middle class, while most black people were left out. The trades offered at the local high schools served as a bridge to close the economic gap between black and white families back then. Nowadays, black people have to go into debt to make economic strides in this country, because trade schools and colleges cost thousands of dollars to attend, and even with a college degree, educated black folks have not seen any equilibrium in the job market and their salaries. It doesn't matter what we do or how many degrees we earn, because society keeps moving the marker every time black folks start to attain success. When most jobs in all major fields started to require a college degree, black women lined up to earn their bachelor's and advanced degrees, only for them to be met with sexism, in addition to racism, as it relates to their earnings, compared to their white male and female counterparts. Being the most educated group of people in America has not served black women well, because they are still fighting for equal pay. However, there are some fields that black women dominate and even the power structure in place can't deny their dominance. Black women are the number one small business owners across America, in spite of all the obstacles set in their path.

While my mom never officially worked full time at a hair salon, but like most talented black women with a hot comb, pair of scissors, and the skills to turn any black woman in her community into a beauty queen in a matter of hours, her kitchen became the fulltime base for many years for a lot of her customers, where she brought out the fabulousness in some of the women from the neighborhood, for a lower fee than what the hair salons would charge them. My mother built an exclusive clientele, and she only worked according to her own schedule while we were kids. She never strayed from her goal of opening a high-end salon, and she would do just that with the assistance of my father.

I was never interested in doing plumbing work, so I joined the military after I graduated from high school, only because I didn't have enough money to pay for college, and I didn't want my college education to become a financial burden upon graduation. Of course, my parents offered to pay for my college education, but I declined. My dad raised me to be my own man and to provide for myself. I wanted to do just that and be my own man. I wasn't even certain whether or not they had the money to fund four years of college for me, but my parents were proud of me and wanted to assist me with anything I wanted to do, in order to become a better person and a productive member of society. I was their pride and joy when I graduated from high school, but they always wanted more for me. My brother, Jeff, made it clear that he wanted to work with my dad, while my sister, Cynthia, was hell-bent on pursuing a degree in business administration in college, so she can help take the family businesses to the next level. I'd gotten accepted to many colleges, but my funds were short, as far as scholarships were concerned. I was always studious and a very good student in school, but my research on scholarships before I graduated from high school fell a little short, and I was a little too late because my guidance counselor at the high school didn't provide us with the resources to help ease the college application process. They were always pushing the black students toward the armed forces and trade schools. Their prejudiced minds couldn't fathom they were creating college-bound students. Being a procrastinator also didn't help my situation. The few scholarships I received for college would've still put me in debt financially after graduation. The military was my next best option, in order to get a free college education.

My father had raised me to be very independent and to always be an Alpha, so putting the financial burden of my education on my parents was never an option. I watched my parents work their asses off, in order to provide for us. The last thing I wanted was to place my own financial burden on them. Besides, there were two more siblings coming up behind me, and I knew they would want to help them as well. My sister was the princess of the three of us, and I had no problem with that. Both, my brother and I were protective of my sister, and we treated her like the princess of the family. I wanted my parents to help her as much as possible, when she was ready to attend college, more than anything. They were even willing to take a second mortgage on their home to help finance my education, but I was completely against it, because becoming my own man or a grownup, was very important to me. I was lucky since I didn't have the responsibilities that my parents had after they'd graduated from high school. I had no child to care for because my parents made sure I didn't repeat their mistakes. They constantly talked to me about sex and ingrained the struggles of raising a child in my mind when I was in high school, and made sure that I protected myself when I became sexually active. In addition, as the eldest child of three, I wanted to establish my own path and set an example for my younger siblings to follow. My parents also did a great job discussing sex with me by the time I was a freshman in high school. They made me aware of all the things that I needed to do to avoid being a young father. Though my parents always provided for us, I also recognized it was time for my dad to take a breather from working so hard. I wanted him to slow down on the overtime at work. That man was dedicated to his family, and he went to great lengths to make sure we never went without.

I truly came from a stable and loving family and home. I'm not saying our pedigree is perfect, but I was raised in a good enough environment to know better and do better. My siblings and I are close, and we never spend a week without reaching out to one another, when I was in the military. I knew that my younger siblings looked up to me, so I made it my duty to set the best example for them, and to make my parents proud. My dad expected me to lead. He raised me in a way that I had no choice but to be the responsible older brother who set the best example possible for my younger siblings. Whenever I was slipping, my dad would remind me that there were two people behind me looking up to me, and aspired to be just like their big brother. I was very mindful of that, because I looked up to my father that way. Not a lot of kids from our neighborhood made it out successfully. Though we didn't live in the roughest part of town, it was still the hood, and we had to deal with hood shit on a daily basis. It was still survival of the fittest, even though we lived in a house. Some people weren't fit to survive in that environment. Fortunately, my parents were there to make sure we kept our focus and made something of our lives.

Before I even thought about bringing Candace home to meet my family, I already knew my parents were going to love her. While Candace would be welcomed with open arms by my entire family, as a daughter and sister in law because of her effortless assimilation into American culture as a first generation American born citizen from immigrant parents, I didn't think it would be as easy when my parents had to meet her parents. My parents still had their own shortcomings, when it came to foreign black people. Some black immigrants are very prejudiced toward African-Americans, and my parents experienced some of it when they were in high school, and while out and about. Not to say that my parents didn't display their own prejudices toward immigrant black people, but I was willing to bridge that gap because Candace was that important to me. Besides, there was no way that they could tell Candace wasn't just plain old African- American, which also would've been a problem, because my mom would've felt comfortable to spew her anti-immigrant sentiments in her presence. However, Candace's parents were a different story, because of their thick Caribbean accents. As a kid, I used to hear my mom say some things that weren't so nice about black immigrants. There were times when my dad would correct her, and there were times that he just didn't say anything because he was tired of correcting her. I have to say that she has evolved over the years, especially after opening her own salon and having to deal with her Caribbean and African clients. Still, sometimes a leopard can't change her spots. Generally speaking, a lot of black people are full of prejudices against their own fellow black men and women, which reinforces division among us. This behavior was learned from white people, who constantly act racist toward black people and immigrants openly in this country. This is the barrier I was going to have to break with my own family, if I had to, because I was not going to break-up with Candace under any circumstances. I knew the cultural norms and customs would prove to be a topic of discussion that would make both parties, but especially my mom, uncomfortable. That's another story on its own, but we'll get to that later. As long as I was happy, that's all my family really cared about at the end of the day. I knew that.

A REGRETFUL DECISION

"Babe, we should take the kids out to the park for some fresh air. They've been cooped up in this house for too long. We don't want them to lose their minds. I'm starting to lose my damn mind myself. Reading a long list of books by black authors, from Black Skin White Mask by Frantz Fanon, to The New Jim Crow by Michelle Alexander and many others in between, and learning our black history to expand our minds and broaden our horizon as a family, and to have the kids write reports on every book they've read so far, has been fine and exhausting at the same time. That's all we've been doing these last few months during the Coronavirus. We have to break this routine, even if it's for a little while. The learning part of it is great, but the kids need a break, and we need a break. We can't allow Covid-19 to make complete cowards out of us. We need a breather from all this," Candace said to me, almost pleading on behalf of the family. As her husband, I turned proudly to my wife, and looked into her eyes, before carefully responding to her suggestion. "You know what, babe? You're right. The kids need a break from the house and their daily routines. It's bad enough we both have been working from home since Covid started, but we can't keep holding our children hostage in this house. And we can't continue to condemn ourselves to this home confinement, which seems almost like an eternity to the kids. The entire family needs some fresh air, and we're not going to limit ourselves to just the backyard today for some fresh air. Get everyone ready, so we can go to the park for a family picnic. Just make sure everyone is wearing their masks, please," I said to her. My wife smiled from ear to ear, before jumping up to give me a hug and a big kiss. I had been so frightful of Covid-19, primarily because of the disparity and the deadly threat the contagion posed specifically in the Black community, according to what was being spread in the media.

Every media outlet had been sonically repeating the same chorus in their reporting on the high infection rate among black folks, and that we were the most susceptible and affected by Covid-19. I wanted to possibly and carefully do everything in my power to protect my family, whether it was propaganda or truth. My wife and my two sons were all that I lived for. As a man, husband, and father, I love my family and will do anything to protect them. This picnic at the park was a much-needed reprieve for my family. We were all looking forward to getting out the house. Candace was more than happy to share the excitement with our twin boys, Dessalines and Toussaint , right after I mentioned the outing. "Boys, go take a shower, we're gonna go to the park for a picnic today!" she yelled from the bottom of the stairs on the first floor of our two-story home. Our 11-year-old twins were excited that they were finally getting out of the house. "Mom, are you serious? Does daddy know about this?" Dessalines enquired. "Fo real, fo real? Does dad know that you're taking us to the park?" Toussaint chimed in, worried that my wife had made the decision without my consent because they knew full and well how worried I had been about Covid, and how overprotective I had been of the family. "Don't worry, your daddy is fully aware, and he's standing right here next to me, and he's coming along, too," my wife answered. "Thanks, Mom! Thanks, Dad!" the two boys yelled in unison, with exhilaration in their voices. I just wanted to see my family happy and felt the need to protect them at all cost at the same time. I didn't hide my fear of Covid-19 from my family, because at first, I had no idea what this epidemic was about, and Dr. Fauci didn't help, with all his lies and flip-flopping all over our television screen daily with his new discoveries. There was always breaking news and a press conference where Dr. Fauci was constantly contradicting himself. The boys couldn't believe that I actually agreed to go outside in public, beyond the limits of our backyard. Even in the backyard, I carried a Lysol spray with me at all times, and constantly disinfected the air around my family, though the next door neighbor was well over 50 yards away. I wasn't taking any chances. As far as the media was concerned, it was a contagion we could just inhale anywhere, and I was doing everything to keep us in that bubble. An airborne disease is the scariest type because once it invades the lungs, that's all she wrote. The safety of my family was my top priority.

In retrospect, I should've gone with my gut feelings and kept the boys in the house that day, but I decided to throw caution to the wind. I went against my gut instincts, and my family ended up paying the price for it on that very day. You can't protect and please your family at the same time. Sometimes tough decisions have to be made, and I should've stood my ground as the head of the family to make sure they were protected. My love for my family was the reason I decided to take them to the park that day, but our lives would forever change, and things will never be the same again. This was the one decision I wish I could take back. In life, there's no restart button, so I have had to live with the consequences of that decision forever. My poor wife can't even cope anymore.

CANDACE AND I

My wife and I have been together for fourteen years now, and married for twelve years. We met back in college. We have always made our immediate family a priority, meaning myself, my wife, and our children. There's always been an order of hierarchy in our home, I'm the king and she's the queen. The two boys are our little princes, and my job as a husband and father is to provide, protect and care for my wife and children in every way possible. It's also my job to teach my children the proper discipline, morality, work ethic, and humility, so they could grow up to be responsible men, while my wife does all of the nurturing. My wife has never interfered with the way that I've raised the boys since we got married. She's always been supportive and understood that I always want what's best for my family. I also trust that she feels the same way and wants the best for our family as well. She never challenges my decisions regarding the family, unless they need to be challenged, provided a viable reason is given, which most of the time, we end up agreeing upon. My household is not run like a dictatorship. My wife's input is very important in every decision that is made for the family, and sometimes we take into consideration the opinions and feelings of our boys as well. It's not an autocracy in the household. My wife is usually very fair in her assessment of the family's needs. We usually consult with each other when big decisions have to be made. I've never been a tyrant or a dictator when it came to my family. I always lead with an open mind. I understand decisions have to be made by one parent sometimes, and some decisions require the input of both of us, in order for us to be in compliance with each other. We both have had our own personal good and bad experiences while growing up, so we decided to keep the good that we learned and throw away the bad, that was detrimental to our upbringing, when we both make decisions regarding our family. Our goal has always been to improve upon the parenting jobs that our own parents did with us. I would describe our parenting skills as modern with a touch of old school. We don't believe in corporal punishment, so we don't beat, whip, or hit our children. We learned very early on as parents there are multiple ways to discipline our children, and beating them is an obsolete and ineffective approach. We are no longer slaves, and we will not treat our children as such.

My parents raised me to respect my wife, and she was raised to respect her husband. Mutual respect was an intricate part of my parents' relationship that I was exposed to. My mom never disrespected my dad, and my dad reciprocated the same courtesy. Even when my parents disagreed, we could never tell as children. Even now in our adult years, they always present a pleasant and united front. I'm not sure if my parents have lived in bliss their entire marriage, but they've managed to play their parts so well that I think all of us, me and both of my siblings, have been fooled into believing that our parents have had the best relationship in the world. They were not the Cosbys by any means, but they damn sure were close pretenders who fooled their children into believing they were the perfect couple. Nah, I can't take a stab like that at my parents, even when I'm joking. My folks are genuine. I'm not trying to duplicate the type of relationship that my parents had, but I want to emulate as much of the good in their relationship as possible. My wife and I have been happy for the most part. We may have small disagreements every now and then over trivial bullshit, but we never go to bed angry with each other. We usually make up before we fall asleep. Making up with my wife is always worth the argument because we go extra hard and extra passionate with our lovemaking. I love this woman with every breath in my lungs.

After serving a couple of tours in Iraq and Afghanistan, as a member of the United States' Marine Corps, I came home and met the love of my life, Candace Joseph, while I was a student at Georgia Tech, studying computer science technology. She came into my life when I least expected it. I had always been a cerebral child, and my goal was to one day become a rich techie with my own start-up. The brainpower was always there, but I didn't take the traditional route that most people tend to take to achieve their goals. I was a little older than the traditional college student because I had just served 4 years in the military. After gaining admission to Georgia Tech, I set out to accomplish my goal of becoming a computer engineer. My GI Bill money came in handy, but it wasn't enough to cover the total cost of tuition at Georgia Tech and room and board. I had to take on a full-time job as head of security at a private security firm that provided security for banks. After all, I was a grown man, and adulting was unavoidable, even though I was a college student. Going back home to Boston was not really an option. I wanted to leave Boston right after high school to start fresh elsewhere. However, after leaving the military, I had to first figure out my options. It was time for me to be a man, and I needed to be away from home to do that. Atlanta ended up on my radar after taking a trip with a friend in the military who was from Atlanta. I was impressed right away with so many progressive black people in one place. It was normal for us to hang out at a restaurant, a bar, the park, or any other place for that matter in Atlanta, where black folks were fully and completely represented. There are so many businesses owned by people that looked like me, I thought I was in black heaven. I really enjoyed that. That was not customary where I'm from in Boston. Most of the nightspots and restaurants in Boston, if not all, are owned by white people, especially around the downtown area, because the city's racist practices make it difficult for black people to get business and liquor licenses for the downtown Boston area. Not only are they difficult to get, but the cost of that liquor license is astronomical, and out of reach for most black business owners, in addition to those liquor licenses being grandfathered to a lot of white business owners. I had to get out of there. I decided Atlanta, Georgia, was going to be my new city of residence.

I was able to secure a one-bedroom apartment not too far from the Georgia Tech campus, in nearby southeast Atlanta. After saving much of my salary while serving in the military, I was able to buy myself a moderately used Toyota Camry, and paid cash for it when I moved to Atlanta. When I say serve, please understand that I mean it in the most subjective way possible. I'm fully aware that the US government doesn't appreciate the service of its citizens, whether black, brown, white, women or other. However, there's a history of black veterans being totally disrespected and overlooked throughout this country's history. In no way would I ever call myself a patriot of a country that doesn't respect and protect its black citizens and continues to be very innovative with their tactics and policies for the endless marginalization, oppression, and subjugation of black people. Besides the obvious racist obstacles that were in my path during my time in the military, everything else in my life was going according to plan. I had a decent job to pay the bills, I was enrolled in school, and my spirit was high. And then it happened....

I was on my way to class one day when I laid eyes on this beautiful goddess that I had no idea would later become the love of my life. She was in her sophomore year at Georgia Tech, enrolled in the School of Public Policy, and barely 19 years old, but she walked with an aura of maturity that caught my attention. She was conservatively dressed in a pair of blue fitted jeans, a black sweater, a pair of black boots, a book bag hanging over her right shoulder, and a couple of textbooks in her hands. The book bag looked quite heavy and filled tightly with books, and she was nonchalantly carrying a heavy load that seemed to have become routine, a natural daily saddle on her shoulder. I wanted to help alleviate whatever burden that book bag was placing on her shoulder like a gentleman would, so I approached her. "Hi, Miss, can I please help take that load off your shoulder today? I would like to carry your book bag to class for you, or wherever it is that you're going," I said, in the most cordial way possible. After the words escaped my mouth, I realized how corny I sounded. "Do you always ask strange women to carry their book bags for them?" she retorted with a slight, but concerted attitude. "Not really, only this beautiful lady standing in front of me, who seems to be exhausting her shoulder right now when an able body man like myself is offering his services for free. I want to rid your shoulder of the pain these heavy books are causing, even if only for a few minutes. I wouldn't want you to hurt your beautiful shoulder. I feel my assistance may be needed at this time," I said flirtatiously, feeling like I had inherited the sense of humor of Chris Rock. "I'm good. I can handle myself. I'm a big girl. I've been here for a couple of years now, and I do this every day. I'll manage," she told me. "I'm sure you will. I just want to ease the load for you, even if it's just this one time. That's all," I told her with an encouraging smile. After I flashed my pearly whites, she eased up a bit. "Do I look that gullible for you to think that a corny line like that would work on me?" she asked. I was a little surprised by her words because her conservative demeanor didn't match her sassiness. Besides, I didn't think I was extra corny, just corny enough. I had to rebound from being a corn-ball real quick.

Candace was a natural beauty with short kinky hair, medium flawless brown skin, full lips, oval eyes, a roundish cute nose, and a beautiful broad smile. In addition, she was very curvy and shapely, but not too over the top. Her radiant beauty was breathtaking, and I just couldn't help myself. As a former military man, I wasn't shy nor abrasive or anything like that, but I was confident. It might've seemed as if my approach toward her was well orchestrated and planned, but everything was really genuine and spontaneous. It all came to me when I laid eyes on her. I don't know or can't recall if I had ever approached a woman that way in my life. She looked that ravishing to me, so I was outside of myself. I instinctively wanted to talk to her. "I don't think you're gullible at all, Miss. I just want to help out a beautiful queen. My name is Kane, Kane Black, but my close friends call me KB," I said, as I extended my hand to greet her.

She looked me up and down, without giving me the side eye, before extending her hand to shake mine, while uttering, "My name is Candace, Candace Joseph. My friends call me Candace, and Ms. Joseph, if you're fresh." She spoke back, I thought to myself. At least I felt like I broke the ice. "Ms. Joseph, huh? I like that. Okay, Ms. Joseph, do you mind if I carry your book bag, as I walk you to your next class?" I asked again. "Actually, my next class is not for another hour and a half. I'm on my way to the library," she told me. "Why waste such a beautiful day inside of a library, when we can be out here getting to know each other? This beautiful lawn is calling our names right now. Let's not allow these white folks to take complete ownership of this beautiful sun and grass that belong to nature and all its members. Black folks can lounge in the sun, too, you know? We's free now," I said jokingly. She chuckled a little at my corny joke, and then started taking inventory of my looks, frame, swag, and everything that encompasses the man who stood before her.

She gazed upon my 5'11 overly toned muscular frame, infectious smile, straight white teeth, low military style faded haircut, strong African features, deep dimples, high cheekbones, and my dark complexion, which was glowing under the sun, before she let out somewhat of a flirtatious smile. I could tell she thought I was attractive, but she didn't want to lead on with any admiration for my aesthetics right away. However, I had a hunch. I caught her staring me dead in my face a couple of times, which was a pure giveaway that she was attracted to me. I was never the ugly duckling ever since I had reached puberty, so I had a sense about myself physically. Before puberty, I heard all the dumb jokes about my dark complexion from grown black colorists and other children who had nothing better to do but find flaws in the dark charcoal color of my skin. However, my parents raised me with the confidence to know better. Knowledge of self was reinforced daily at my house. Being dark was my special gift to the world, but being handsome was inherited from my mom and dad. I was casually dressed in a pair of blue jeans, long sleeve v-neck sweater, and sneakers. It was fall season in Atlanta, and the weather was perfect. "Boy, I've got work to do. Don't nobody wanna be out here laying in the sun with these white folks. I'm trying to graduate out of here in another three years with a master's degree," she told me. I believed she might've hinted at the fact that she was enrolled in the five-year master's program at the school, but I wasn't sure just yet. I assumed her goal was to complete her bachelor's and master's degrees in five years, and she would soon let me know how determined she was to meet that goal during our conversation. "Well, I'm only in my first semester here. I'm just trying to navigate college life," I told her. "You're a freshman? Boy, I don't date men that are younger than me," she revealed with a smirk on her face. Right away, I saw the opening to her softer side. "So, you've thought about dating me, even for a sec? Those words didn't just roll off your tongue. You were thinking that I'm dating material. Besides, who said I was younger than you? Maybe I'm just a late bloomer," I said to her sarcastically. My youthful looks didn't always work to my advantage. There have been times when I've gone out with my friends I couldn't get in a bar or a club without proper ID. "Well, you need to take your wannabe late blooming Lance Gross looking behind somewhere else. I've got to make my way to the library to get some work done," she told me. Comparing my looks to Lance Gross' was something that I had grown accustomed to over the years. Everyone in the army used to always bring up Lance Gross' name whenever they wanted to crack a funny joke about me. I was just happy and lucky the brother was a sex symbol to a lot of women. "Can I at least carry your bag to the library for you?" I asked again. "Since you keep insisting...sure," she said while handing me the bag off her shoulder. That bag was fucking heavy, and my arm almost fell out of the damn socket when she handed it to me. I didn't anticipate that shit to be so heavy. That woman was strong, I thought. She made carrying that heavy ass bag look so effortless, though. The library was a few blocks up the road on campus, so I had plenty of time to put in a few words, to see if I could convince her to give me her number.

The breezy fall air mounted our faces in the most pristine way, as we strolled toward the library. I was feeling kind of lucky and even feeling myself a little, that she had allowed me to walk her to the library. It was almost a pubescent-like moment, but that's exactly what happens when the love bug suddenly takes over the soul sometimes. It brings the child out in all of us. I felt like I was in a candy store in Candace's presence and she was all the candy I needed. My next class wasn't for another hour and a half, so I had plenty of time to kill in between. While the campus may have been crowded with students, I felt as if I were on an isolated island alone with Candace. I kept gazing at her unbelievable beautiful almond eyes, and kept filling my head up with thoughts that were too premature to even mention right now. Not perverted thoughts, though, just happy thoughts of being with Candace forever. A little fantasy, if you will, about her being my one and only forever. I truly believe most men know when a woman is the one, upon first meeting her. That's how I felt about Candace when I first laid eyes on her. "What made you choose Georgia Tech?" I asked her, in the midst of our stroll. "I've always wanted to live in Washington DC or Atlanta. I'm originally from New York. Howard University was my first choice, but the financial package they gave me barely covered my tuition, so I chose Georgia Tech. It was the perfect school for me to earn my bachelor's and master's degrees in Public Policy, while living among my people. Chocolate city, baby," she said to me with enthusiasm. She finally confirmed she was working on both, a bachelor's and master's degrees. While she was talking, I was taking inventory of her entire body, demeanor, her sexy strut, her New York accent, and even the tone of her voice. "Well, I consider myself lucky that you chose Georgia Tech, otherwise, I wouldn't have met you," I told her. "Don't consider yourself so lucky just yet. One of the reasons I came here, is because I enjoy being around my own people, especially since they're doing so well here. I'm focused, determined and wanna do just as well as I see these successful black business owners and entrepreneurs doing in a few years in Atlanta," she let me know bluntly. "I like that. You're supposed to be focused and determined. You see, we already have two things in common," I said in a humorous tone. "Okay, Mr. Black, we're gonna have to see about that," she let out in a serious tone.

After she made the comment about not dating a person younger than her, I started to think my youthful-looking face was a gift and a curse. I hadn't aged much since I graduated from high school, but I had gained about twenty pounds of muscle since joining the military. My mature and grown face hadn't yet developed. I still had a youthful face, so she naturally thought I was an 18 year-old freshman. I wanted to clear the air about my age so she could see me as an option for dating. I quickly segued into what I thought was an important subject to her, HBCUs. "Howard University was one of my top choices too, but their financial package fell way short for me as well. You said degrees, huh?" I inquired. "Yes, degrees. I'm enrolled in the five-year program that allows me to get both, my bachelor's and master's degrees in exactly 5 years, but I might try to do it a semester sooner," she reinforced. "What part of New York are you from?" I asked. "I'm from the Saint Albans section of Queens. Have you ever been to New York?" she asked. "Of course,

I have family all over New York. Some of them are in Queens, and even more in Long Island and Brooklyn," I told her. Candace started to show a little more interest as I divulged more about myself and my background. "What brought you to Georgia Tech?" she asked. "Well, I was in the military for 4 years. I just came home after serving my last tour in Afghanistan. I've always been interested in computers, and Georgia Tech offered the best flexibility possible, according to hectic my schedule. I decided to make the best use of my GI Bill here. I was stationed at the Marine Corps Logistics Base in Albany, GA. After my 4 years were up, I decided to move to Atlanta. I'm originally from Boston," I told her. "Interesting... A military man, huh? Don't military men practice infidelity like it's a religion?" she asked. I quickly took a couple of steps back from her, threw my hands up in the air, before sighing and responding with, "Wow! I had to run from under that big blanket statement you just threw out there. That was the most prejudiced statement if I've ever heard one. No, we're not all alike, and not all military servicemen are cheaters. The military actually teaches loyalty, but not everyone choose to follow their teachings. People in every sector of society cheat. It's not exclusive to military people. I have never cheated on anybody, and any man who would dare cheat on a beautiful woman like you, must be out of his mind," I said to her, with a smile, the best confidence I could muster, and honesty. I could tell she felt that I was genuine in my reply to her statement. I let her know that I thought highly of her, even though we had just met. I knew that most women enjoy being around men who are respectful, and I wanted to show Candace the utmost respect for taking the time to talk to me. My father taught me a long time ago that a woman is as delicate as a flower and that she must be watered carefully in order for her to bloom properly, just as he'd been watering my mom for years throughout their marriage. My pops taught me how to be a gentleman, he led by example. I was also trying to maximize my opportunity with Candace. I couldn't afford to waste time and opportunity.

"I wasn't talking from personal experience per se, but I've heard. I've never dated anybody from the military, but you all's reputation precedes you," she said. "You all? There you go throwing that blanket around again, and I have to dodge it again.(took a couple of steps back for emphasis) You don't know anything yet about my gentleness, kindness, my loving and giving heart, my faithfulness and devotion to the one I'm gonna love, once I fall in love with you. I mean her, once I'm in love with her. That's the only kind of reputation that you're going to discover, and you can only find that out by giving me your number right now," I told her. I couldn't be any more forward, and she kind of liked the fact that I expressed my interest in her without hesitation. "Ok, Mr. Boston, I'm gonna take a chance and give you my number, since I'm single and all. Please don't be a stalker. I can't handle those problems right now," she told me. She was opening up to me, and I wanted to seal the deal, but first, she curiously had to know one thing that I had grown accustomed to hearing from black folks who were not from Boston, "I haven't met too many black people from Boston. Is there a lot of us up there?" She wasn't the first person to ask this question about Boston, even though most of America's black leaders have ties to Boston. From Crispus Attucks, to Dr. Martin Luther King, Malcolm X, Minister Louis Farrakhan and many others, that I would later talk to her about. "Sure. There are plenty of us to go around. You're not gonna find the same amount of black folks in Boston that you would find in New York City or Atlanta, but we have big enough communities in the Metro Boston and Cambridge area. Maybe one day you'll get an opportunity to go home with me, and I can give you a tour of Boston. "Maybe," she said, with a smile. Just like that, I knew I had a chance, as long as I made the best of my opportunity.

By the time Candace and I reached the library, the ice was broken. We spent a few minutes talking, and I walked away with her number, as my happy ass strolled to my next class. My persistence paid off, and her body language didn't hide the fact that the attraction between us was mutual, which kept me hopeful. A couple of weeks after our initial meeting, and spending way too much time talking to one another on the phone, Candace and I planned to go on our first date. There was no big expectation because we were both college students living on a budget. I took her to Gladys

Knight's Chicken and Waffles on Ponce De Leon Avenue in mid-town Atlanta. It was a casual date, just to share a meal with her and to get to know her better face to face again. However, Candace showed up looking like a three-course meal, and sexier way beyond my imagination. Everything was good, though, I wasn't tripping. I had to contain my excitement when I first laid eyes on her at the restaurant. Candace could make any piece of clothing look good. Her body was perfect in every way. She wore a simple dark tan fitted sweater dress and brown boots. That was it. That's all she needed to wear. Less was definitely more, and she pulled it off. I almost lost my damn mind, she looked so sexy. We had decided to meet at the restaurant. Since I arrived before her, I got a chance to take a full view of her sexy strut from the front door toward my table. And I was not the only person taking inventory of Candace's sexy walk, gorgeous body, and beautiful face. I could see other women tugging on the arms of some of the men who seemed lost in Candace's natural cadence. I pulled her chair out for her when she arrived at my table so she could take her seat across from me. Not long after, the waitress glanced over to my table and noticed that she had arrived. She walked over to our table to take our order. Everything on the menu looked good, but we settled for chicken and waffles.

After ordering our food, Candace and I chatted about a few things while we waited for our food to arrive. We also ordered drinks. She settled for lemonade, because she wasn't old enough to drink liquor, but it was all cool because I also ordered lemonade. We talked about almost everything, including the cities where we grew up, our likes and dislikes, our family traditions, and upbringing. To me, it was a perfect date. The physical and intellectual chemistry between us was undeniable. I wanted to leave the impression of a perfect gentleman, so I didn't even try to kiss her, even though I really wanted to. I also knew there would be a second date, a third date, and a fourth date in the future, based on our interaction and chemistry. There was no way she wasn't going to call me again. I could feel it in my soul when we met that she would be permanent in my life. Our first date only confirmed my intuition about her. Candace and I became inseparable for months after our first date, until we couldn't resist being apart from each other anymore.

It had been a few months, and I wanted to do something special for Candace, but I wanted to wait for a special occasion, because I didn't want to appear overly eager and thirsty. It just so happened that Valentine's Day was coming up, and I used that as an opportunity to make my move. To be honest, I really don't give a damn about these retail holidays. My lady will be special to me 365 days of the year.

Valentine's Day had crept upon us in no time, and I wanted to win Candace's heart once and for all. I needed to go all out, so she could understand how I serious I was about her. It had been about six months since we had been seeing each other, and I wanted Candace to be fully aware of how strong and true my feelings had grown for her. I knew she was going to be my forever from the moment I laid eyes on her. I can't really explain it, but it was just a gut feeling I had with certainty. Then again, it could've just been instincts. I've never been clairvoyant in any way, but I was definitely certain about her. Still, I had no idea how long it would take before Candace would realize I was the one for her. Maybe she knew it, too? My feelings were simply growing for her, and I didn't want to impose anything on her. I needed her to move at her own pace. Love can't be rushed. It has to take its natural course. She was working part-time as the front desk receptionist at the W Hotel in Atlanta during the time we met. She worked from 6-10:00 PM on Fridays, 9 AM-5 PM, on Saturdays and 12-6 PM on Sundays while she focused on school during the week. Luckily, Valentine's Day fell on a Saturday the year that we met. I had to plan carefully, in order to make sure my surprise for Candace went accordingly. I'd enlisted the help of one of Candace's co-workers, in order to gain easier access to a room that I had paid for at the hotel, so I could lay out my plans, which included a set of black matching bras and panties, a beautiful black dress, red pumps, and a bottle of Chanel No. 5. All of the items were laid on the bed for Candace to see, with a note detailing everything that I wanted her do. Even though I had been planning all of it in my head, I felt it was somewhat impromptu as well, because I waited last minute to put it together so Candace wouldn't discover my plans. I was hoping that Candace would be game for my thoughtfulness. I kept my fingers crossed and hoped for the best. She was a little perturbed when her co-worker handed a keycard to her for access to a room that was located on the fourth floor after her shift was over. However, I was told that her confusion soon turned to glee, after the coworker explained that I had paid for the room and there was a surprise waiting for her. I didn't want her to think that I just wanted to have her in a hotel room by myself to take advantage of her, which is why I approached it the way that I did. I'm not gonna lie and say that I would turn down the opportunity to rock Candace's world, but I just didn't want her to be aware of it.

I imagined when she walked in the room to find the items that I had laid on the bed for her she would be pleasantly surprised. That's the reaction I kept hoping for and crossed my fingers that it would manifest. This was the first time I had ever planned anything like that. I really had no expectations. I also didn't want to offend her by making her believe that all I wanted was to sleep with her. I just wanted to treat her to a great night. There was no rolling of any dice, or any hope that she would jump my bones, but I did put in the efforts to set up the occasion. I wanted Candace to feel special, because as college students, we constantly had schoolwork on our minds and nothing else. Whether or not Candace would want me to be in the room with her, it would be ultimately her decision. However, this would be the very first time we were going to spend a night together, and I didn't hold my breath that she was going to go along with my plans. Based on the trajectory of our relationship, I thought it might work. I had sneaked into the room through the back entrance earlier to bring a little makeup bag, deodorant, body wash, accessories and the whole nine that she needed to get ready. I was very well-versed in her favorite hygiene products. I paid attention. I used to watch and took notes of the products she used to wash her face, her body, and the brands of lipstick and eyeliner she used. I went shopping online a couple of weeks earlier to make sure I got all the items that were necessary for my surprise, and I definitely planned meticulously. I bought all these items just to make sure she wouldn't need for anything. Candace didn't normally wear makeup anyway, but this was going to be a special night. She also didn't make a big deal of her hair. As a college student, she couldn't really afford to be at anybody's hair salon every other week anyway, so she wore her hair natural. I'm glad she wore her natural hair because I couldn't imagine her any other way. I was given 2 sets of keycards for access to the room by the front desk clerk, when I made the reservation at the hotel. I left a key for Candace and took one with me. By the time Candace got off work, she was way more than excited to follow my directives in the note that I left for her. She went upstairs to the room, took a shower, and got ready. I arrived promptly at 7:15 PM to pick her up, which allowed me enough time for the 30 minute drive to the restaurant located downtown. The reservation was set for 8:00 PM. Since we were both fans of

Thai food, I chose this upscale Thai restaurant in Atlanta.

Candace looked like a Hollywood starlet when she opened the door to let me in the room. In my head, I was thinking, "Let's skip dinner, because you look like a three-course meal, and I want to eat it all right now," but I knew better. Candace needed to be treated like a lady and very special that night. She stood there in that little black wrap-around dress that I picked out, red pumps, a red purse in her hand, flawless makeup, smelling like the roses from her bottle of Chanel No 5 perfume that I'd purchased for her, and a bright smile on her face. Before stepping in to hug her, I brought my right hand from behind my back to hand her a dozen roses that I picked up from the flower shop. She reached for them, and gave me a long kiss. She wasn't too concerned about messing up her lipstick. I had a feeling this was going to be a magical night, and I wanted everything to be perfect. I didn't skip a beat either when I got dressed. She took inventory of my lengthy muscular frame wrapped in a medium-blue 2-piece suit, a baby blue shirt, light brown shoes, and belt to match. I didn't disappoint with my Aqua Di Gio cologne by Georgio Armani. My aroma was definitely edible, just like her aroma was delectable to me. She inhaled my cent and whispered in my ear, "You almost make me want to skip whatever it is that you have planned for me. I think I want what's in front of me right now." Her flirting got me acting like a little nervous child. Candace wanted to hold me a little longer, as she hugged and inhale my scent for a few minutes more. This cologne complemented my body perfectly, but we had to go, because I felt a bulge coming on, and she could feel it, too. Time was of the essence, and we needed to make it to the restaurant on time. CPT (Colored people time) wasn't an option. Otherwise, the very busy restaurant would cancel our reservation on Valentine's night. The busiest night for all restaurants around the world was nothing to play with.

The drive to the restaurant was joyous and pleasant, as Candace thanked me for being so thoughtful by making the day special for her. She hadn't even gotten to the main course yet, because I had more in store for her. When we arrived at the restaurant, the environment from the exterior alone was inviting. We looked around to see the dimly lit garden to the side and couples sitting on the patio surrounded by heat lamps, which created the perfect cozy romantic environment before we even set foot in the restaurant. I had never done this before. She was seeing a different side of me. After all, I was only the second man she'd ever dated, and the first one was just a puppy crush who thought taking her to the movies and Applebee's was the best thing ever. I surmised this from the information she revealed to me about her last relationship throughout our conversations. I was on my grown man shit! Pulling up to the upscale restaurant and handing my keys to the valet alone, was something she had never experienced with a man during a date. Of course, her dad had taken her and her mom to nice restaurants with valets and everything before, according to her, but no man had stepped their game up with her the way I did on that Valentine's night. After the valet took my car, he handed me a ticket. We walked inside the restaurant to meet the Maitre D at the front. He checked our name to confirm the reservation and then walked us to a corner booth. After we sat down, Candace and I stared into each other's eyes for a few minutes, before even thinking about looking at the menu that the Maitre D handed us. She reached for my hands and squeezed them in a manner that felt like a body hug. I returned the favor. It was at that moment we both realized we were falling for one another. "I've been looking forward to this night all week long. I wanted to do something special for you," I whispered to her while gazing into her eyes. "I appreciate all your effort. You're a very thoughtful man. You're making it very difficult for me to ignore my feelings for you," she whispered back. In the middle of a crowded restaurant with patrons sitting not too far from us, Candace and I felt like we were alone on a quiet island. Our surroundings didn't matter, as we focused on each other and savored the moment we were spending together.

A few minutes had gone by and we were still acting like two lost lovebirds, completely oblivious to the menu the Maitre D had handed to us. A young waitress showed up to ask if we were ready to order. Candace and I were shaken out of our stupor and decided to grab the menus to see what else we could have, beside each other.

"Can you give us a few more minutes, please?" Candace politely asked the waitress. "Sure. Take your time. Would you like something to drink in the meantime?" she asked. "Babe, what would you like to drink?" I asked Candace. "Water will be fine," she told the waitress. "I'll have the same thing as well," I said. Since Candace wasn't old enough to drink yet, I didn't want to put her in a position to feel left out, so I ordered water, but the occasion definitely called for some wine. Besides, I had a nice bottle of wine on ice waiting at the hotel for us to share when we got back. Just because she wasn't twenty-one years old yet, it didn't mean she couldn't celebrate with a glass of wine. I was very inconspicuous with the wine. I knew she wouldn't find it where I hid it in the room. After looking over the menu, Candace settled on basil seafood with white rice, while I opted for the lobster Panang with brown rice. We ordered shrimp rolls as an appetizer. The waitress came back with the appetizer fairly quick. Candace and I looked like a couple in love, as we fed each other the rolls. After each dip into the sweet and sour sauce, we would open our mouths, so we could feed each other a piece of the shrimp roll. It was cute. The main course arrived moments later. The conversation over a great meal was even better, as I learned a few more things about Candace, her family and upbringing. She was delighted to know that my parents had been married for almost twenty-five years. She knew that they had set the bar high and provided a pretty great example for me to follow. We took our time to savor our food. It was all delicious. We ate off each other's plates like an old married couple. After we were done eating, I paid for dinner and left a hefty tip for the waitress who was patient and kind to us throughout dinner.

We stepped outside and I handed the valet my ticket to retrieve my car. I held the door open for Candace on the passenger's side, while the valet held the door open for me on the driver's side. I handed him a couple of dollars for tip, before taking off. On the drive back to the hotel, things would heat up in the car, unbeknownst to me. As I maneuvered my way behind the wheel toward the expressway, Candace's hand slowly found my inner thighs, and she started rubbing me in the most sensual way. Candace had never made the first move on me before, but it was a pleasant surprise. I was doing everything in my power to stay focused on the road, while at the same time trying to speed up to my destination, without getting victimized by a cop's speed trap. Valentine's Day in Atlanta is famous for the cops handing out more tickets than their quota requires. I guess working on Valentine's Day and leaving their own spouses at home can force some of them to forget that it's supposed to be a night for lovers. Damn, those haters! I normally keep my black ass home on Valentine's Day, because I never really cared for the day. However, since this relationship was fresh, I needed to do something nice to woo Candace. I could've done this for her on any day, though. I was vigilant while driving, as I paid attention to the road, and at the same time trying to control the blood flow in my pants. Candace was pretty certain of the reaction she received from me when her hand inadvertently touched the veins across the monstrous blood-filled tool in my pants. She slowed her hand down on it, to admire its length and girth. I've been known to carry more than my fair share and perhaps a little more handful than Candace expected. She was more than amused, and seemed like she was looking forward to climbing the mountain that her river was running wild for. One good turn deserves another, I thought, as Candace boldly played with my hardened tool. My excitement was about to burst right through my pants, if she continued the sensual manual massage she unleashed on me. My head was filled with anticipation of great lovemaking all night. I kept my eyes focused on the road to avoid a premature embarrassing situation, with my left hand on the wheel, while my right hand slid down to Candace's inner thighs, in order to shift the focus of attention on her. I swear she almost had me for a minute. I came this close to busting a quick one in the car, I was sure my premature ejaculation would've led to an early night abruptly. No woman wants a minute man.

My right hand found comfort and a home between her warm, welcoming, and habitable firm thighs. She started to shake a little, as I glided my hands up and down against her skin, groping as much thigh as I could in the most sensual way. I knew she was more than a little moist, but she tried to contain herself. The bulge in my pants was as inflamed as an irritating bone bruise. My boner needed to bruise the hell out of Candace's kitty cat. I hurried back to the hotel as quickly as I could, without getting pulled over by one of those overzealous Georgia State troopers.

The night was set in motion when I arrived at the hotel. After handing my keys to the valet at the front door of the hotel, I rushed to the other side of the car to open the door for Candace, with anticipation taking over my body. As she stepped out, I held her hand in mine before pulling back and scooping her up from the ground into my awaiting arms to bring her upstairs to the room. Candace was fairly lightweight at 120 lbs, given the fact that I was easily benching 300 lbs at the gym every other day. I wanted to act like her knight in shining armor, as I carried her through the halls of the hotel to the elevator. Other patrons, but especially the women, were envious of my romantic gesture. Whether I was her knight or piece for the night, I felt knighted by her. "Babe, you're gonna need your strength for the rest of the night for what we're about to do, please put me down," she whispered in my ear with a little tongue action on my neck while in the elevator. I got the confirmation that I was eagerly anticipating. It was a matter of me living up to the situation. I knew I wanted to make love to her all night long. After slowly placing Candace back down on her feet, I proceeded to kiss her against the back wall of the elevator, and she reacted passionately to my kiss. It wasn't until the little bell rang in the elevator that we realized we had reached our floor, because we had locked lips the entire way up. Candace was now looking like a meal to the hungry wolf that was me, and I looked like the vulnerable prey that Ms. Predator Candace wanted to take a bite of. We hurried hand in hand and lips to lips down the hallway to our room. I could barely slide my keycard into the door lock. I was a little more than impatient. No, we were both a little more than impatient. After we got in the room, we barely pushed the door closed when I pinned Candace against the door for another long passionate kiss. Our breaths were heavy, as we wrestled our lips and tongues in unison, creating a climatic environment that forced Candace to pull off my shirt and suit jacket and reached for my chiseled bare chest. She touched, kissed and caressed my chest until I developed goose bumps. I stood there helpless, as Candace worked her magic tongue against my washboard stomach and chiseled chest. The light suction on my nipple with her lips sent me into a frenzy that launched my hands aggressively into her bra like I was reaching for a military grenade. I pulled one breast out to allow my tongue to slowly savor her nipple, licking it slightly and ever so lightly, while Candace succumbed to my touch and desires. "I want you," she whimpered in half breaths while reaching for my boner that nearly busted out of my pants. She fondled my crotch as I sucked one of her breasts. Feeling comfortable and desirable, I pulled out her other breast and started alternating between the two with my soft tongue strokes.

The fire between Candace's thighs couldn't be denied, as I

reached down to feel her wetness with my middle finger. I slowly massaged her clit with my finger while I made my way down to her navel, and slowly pulled the string on her dress to undress her. Finally, she stood there before me, body bare, stomach sexy, breasts perky, sexual hunger in her eyes, and craving for me. I was ready to do what I had been waiting to do to her for months now. While kneeling in front of her, I placed one of her legs over my shoulder, planting her heavenly goodies directly in my face, as she held on to my head for the joyous ride she was about to take on my tongue. I motioned my tongue slowly on the tip of her clitoris and whispered, "Damn, you taste good." She really did. The motion of my tongue became more intense, as she let out a moan of approval for my cunnilingus skills. "Eat it, baby. Eat your kitty cat," she said, without realizing her slip of the tongue. She unofficially confirmed it was mine, and it made me even more determined to please her. The motion of my tongue shifted from up and down to circular, and faster. She could barely stand it. Her sensitive clit could bear no more, as she screamed, "I'm cumming! You're making me cum. Damn, baby, don't stop!" She held on tight to my head, as her body quivered over my shoulder. I held on steadfastly to her round ass, while she let out moans of pleasure. It seemed as if Candace needed that relief. I was more than happy to provide it. That was actually the first time a man had made her climax. She'd revealed it to me the moment after it happened. "I never thought it would feel so good to cum," she said. The only boyfriend she'd had, and to whom she'd lost her virginity to during her freshman year in college, was never able to help her reach those heights sexually. He was inexperienced and felt apprehensive about performing oral sex on her. His loss! The level of his immaturity in everything was the reason that Candace ended the relationship with him, in addition to the fact that he thought he was God's gift to all the women on campus, which also didn't help. She was the one who gave him the confidence boost when she agreed to date him, but it all went to his head. Never mind all that.

Round one was good, but I had enough energy for more than one round, and I aimed to please her. Candace was about to discover reactions, emotions, and pleasure from her body that she never knew she could feel. As I eased out of my clothes, Candace lay naked on the bed watching me. It was a real live fantasy happening for her, and me too, because the look in her eyes made it seem like she found me to be completely irresistible and sexy. Only the ancestors knew how irresistible I found her. "I like your chiseled body, and it's giving me a lot of naughty thoughts right now," Candace spoke her mind out loud. "What's he gonna do next with that long thing?" was the pondering look I saw in her eyes, as she stared at me. Candace had no idea that the fantasy was all mine. I had been waiting for this day to make her feel like a Goddess, and I wanted to pour all my love in her. She looked so heavenly. If I wasn't too anxious to have her, I would've gotten on my knees to pray to the ancestors for blessing me with her presence. I eased my way toward her and proceeded to touch her breasts and kiss her all over again. Her temperature had dropped back to normal, but my touch made it rise again immediately. My kisses were soft and her lips were delicious. I wanted to reach her soul with my lovemaking. She felt my desire to please her, and she became moist, anticipating my every move. I might've been a little too patient for her, so she reached out and grabbed for my hardened 10-inch tool and softly wrapped her lips around it. She couldn't resist. By then my hardened tool had extended to its full length and thickness, filled with blood-popping veins, appetizing, and ready to serve and be served. The warmth of her mouth was soothing, sweet, and exhilarating all at once. I hadn't anticipated that treat, so I stood on the edge of the bed to allow my new queen to please me. "Ooh, ahh, mmhhhh," was all I could utter, while Candace worked the magic of her tongue on me. I gazed right into her eyes with a comfortable stare to let her know it was okay for her to love me...for us to love each other. She caressed my shaft with her tongue slowly, while massaging my scrotum with her hand. It was sensual and sexy at the same time. All I could think about at the time was that I was never going to let this woman out of my life. After pleasing me for about ten minutes, I decided to take charge of the situation. It was my turn to take her to seventh heaven once again. I had her lay on her back on the bed and started licking her toes slowly until I licked my way all up to her thighs. My tongue made her shiver, as I hoisted it on her clitoris sensually, while making my way to her erogenous zone. Candace couldn't stand it anymore, and I could sense it.

I wrapped myself in a large Magnum condom and slowly glided inside her wetness, and at that moment, she could feel her cup runneth over. Her abundant flowing juices were obvious. My strokes were sensual and punctual to her erogenous region. "Oh my God!" she exclaimed, while I slowly wind and grind my way inside her. My tongue moved magnificently on her perfect C-cup breasts and nipples. It was double ecstasy. Her breathing was heavy, as I put all my effort into pleasing her like I had never done to a woman before. I was on some next-level shit, because Candace was special. I wanted to make it a night she would never forget. I also didn't want it to be the type of memorable night where I came up short. I slowly eased my way out of her every time I was near climaxing. I was anxious but I was more eager to please her. While I was trying to raise the bar sexually to take her to a climactic state, I locked lips with her to ease the process. Kissing her was more sensual and climactic than anything else to me. Finally, I needed that sexual relief. I held her tightly and kissed her passionately for about ten minutes before releasing in the condom. She reached her climatic plateau in unison with me, so she held on to make sure my destination was reached with the same level of intense pleasure as hers. The two of us lay naked in the bed for about an hour. We sipped on a glass of wine, before going for round three. Candace and I would please one another until dawn, and it was a memorable night that both of us will never forget.

THEREAFTER

During pillow talk, I discovered that Candace, like me, didn't care much for Valentine's Day. "You didn't have to go all out like that because of some made-up holiday these people created for capitalistic reasons. Don't get me wrong, I appreciate all that you've done, but I don't ever celebrate Valentine's Day," she revealed. I wasn't surprised that she didn't care much for Valentine's Day. I should've known that, because we mesh so well in every other way. "I didn't know if you were one of these women who make a big deal of this made-up holiday, so I took my chances," I told her. "You better learn your woman," she said while laughing. "My woman, huh? So it's official, you're my woman?" I asked. "You think I'd do this with just any man. Only a special man who has my heart would get me into this vulnerable position," she declared, with passion in her eyes. "I'm happy to be your man. Say no more. We are now officially an item, I mean a couple," I announced while tripping over my words. Telling me I was her man was the highlight of my night, and the best ecstasy I experienced in my lifetime. "You know I'm gonna love you forever, right?" I mumbled. "You better.

I plan on loving you forever as well," she confirmed.

Soon after our memorable night, we became inseparable. We decided to see each other exclusively from then on, and our love started blooming even more. We were always together, in and out of school, and our relationship developed into a healthy, stable, and loving one, to the point where neither of us wanted to be apart from the other. Candace followed through with her plan to obtain her bachelor's and master's degrees in five years, while I graduated with my bachelor's degree at the same time her master's degree was conferred upon her. After graduation, she was offered a job by the mayor's office, earning a handsome salary. Since she and I were inseparable, we decided to move in together, to the dismay of her parents. However, she wanted to follow her heart. She kept the fact that we lived together a secret from her parents for a while, though. She only agreed to move in with me after I surprised her and asked for her hand in marriage. While I proposed to her after we graduated from college, I wanted to wait until after I had at least a year's worth of work experience before getting married to Candace, and she was fine with that. When we first met, she was living on campus, but she hardly spent any time in her dorm room after we met. She was always at my apartment. The natural progression of our relationship led to our cohabitation for a year, and our marriage would come soon after in 2010. By time Candace had also gained some work experience, and was making plan to eventually start her own business as an independent contractor for the local, state and federal government projects. I was a computer geek, and Candace was passionate about public policy. Her life's goal was to change all the government policies that affect the lives of black people in a negative way. Working with the mayor's office was just the beginning of her journey to change the world.

Our wedding was pretty lit, but there's no need to go into the specific details right now, because there's so much to our story and we also had to overcome some family drama before our union. Our family background differs in some ways, but eventually, we were able to get to a place where our parents understood that our relationship was about us, and not about them. I want to spare you the details of how much a beautiful bride my wife was and how happy we were to walk down the aisle for now, but there was nothing cliché about our wedding. Please best believe that we will never forget the day we tied the knot. Be patient, that part of the story is coming.

A few months after we got married, Candace and I decided to move to the middle class suburbs of Gwinnett County, Georgia, in Snellville, to purchase a home. Gwinnett County is "considered" one of the most diverse counties in Georgia, and we felt comfortable there. We also chose Snellville because of its close proximity to downtown Atlanta, and the fact that their school system is one of the best in Georgia, in addition to the growth of the black middle class in that area. I was able to use my veteran status to secure a VA loan to purchase our first home. We settled on a four-bedroom and two-and-half baths home with a big backyard in Snellville, GA, so that our future children could have enough space to roam around and be free. Snellville offered plenty of opportunities as one of the most diverse cities in close enough proximity to Stone Mountain Park, and it also cut down our commuting time to and from work in Atlanta. Being in Snellville was like getting the best of both worlds.

CANDACE'S EMOTIONAL BLACK HISTORY

My feelings for Kane changed completely after that Valentine's night when he wooed me to the moon and back. Kane was on some grown man shit that I was not used to, and hadn't experienced from any man before him. His bedroom skills are off the charts. I can't even describe the euphoria I went through for a couple of days after being with him. I wanted to have him all the time. I never anticipated that he would go through all that planning to make sure that I had the most memorable Valentine's Day celebration ever. I never thought that Valentine's Day could be so special. Don't get me wrong, he would definitely go on to top that day during the course of our marriage, but I will never forget that night. That was the night that I made up my mind that I wanted to spend the rest of my life with Kane. He was so gentle with me and treated me like a queen during that entire special "unforgettable" once-in-a-lifetime experience eventful night. I felt safe and comfortable in his arms. We had never had sex prior to that night, and

Kane did everything in his power to make sure the moment was as comfortable and sweet as possible for me. Men like him didn't grow on trees, so I decided to hold on to my fruit forever. Kane has made every day feel like Valentine's since we've been together.

Kane also gave me the impression that he was passionate about family and would be a good father if we were to have children one day. All that ran through my mind while he was inside of me, pleasing me with all his might. He had taken me to a place where no man dared to explore before. I saw us way beyond that night, and I knew that he would be in my life forever. However, in the back of my mind, I also knew the cultural differences in our families could create some problems for our relationship. I had never really introduced my parents to anybody that I was dating before, because I never took anybody seriously prior to Kane. Still, I used to listen and hear some of the negative comments and preconceived notions from African-Americans about other black people from foreign countries, based on their distant experiences and interactions with them on the streets and at work. Though I was born in New York, I never forget that I came from a very proud immigrant family from Haiti, and my parents tried as much as they could to instill their Haitian values into me, and passed their work ethic onto me as well. Haitians are resilient and hard-working people, and most Haitian parents always want what's best for their children and family. My mother especially, had issues with some African-Americans, not just because of the stigma and propaganda that she saw on television every day about them, but also because some of them were always quick to try to denigrate her as an immigrant, because of her thick accent whenever she spoke English, and the fact that she actually came from Haiti, an island with a rich history that all black people around the world should be proud of, but only if they knew the true history, not the bullshit narrative constantly being presented by the American media. I guess I can be a little more objective because I was actually born and raised here, and I learned to appreciate the good sides of both, Haitian culture and African-American culture.

Unless I specifically state to someone that I'm Haitian, the first thought most people always have about me, is that I'm African-American, simply because of my blackness or black skin. The US government and the media don't always paint a great image of Haiti as the first free Black Republic in the world, so I can objectively understand how the root of some of the ignorance about Haiti coming from some people can be missed in translation. Prejudice usually keeps us divided, while racism destroys us. It was up to me to make sure my mother's prejudices didn't destroy the relationship I wanted to build with Kane. My father is more pragmatic like me. He always assesses every situation in its entirety and makes sure everything is exclusively relative to the facts, before forming an opinion. My mother was usually opinionated without finding out the true facts. Her factual sources were always the six o'clock news. She would always jump the gun to believe the propaganda and the false narrative displayed on the news every day about African-Americans. However, she would argue and dispute everything they reported about Haiti as false propaganda and fake news with anybody within earshot most of the time, without realizing her own prejudiced way of thinking. She never objectively believed the same propaganda the media used to degrade Haiti could also be used to denigrate African-Americans. Whenever my mother would jump the gun about other black people, I was usually the one to bring her back to reality to see both sides. I tried my best to shed light on things for her, but it didn't always work.

Most Haitian parents are stubborn, and my mother was no different. I knew it would be somewhat of an uphill battle to help bring clarity to my situation. My mother wanted me to marry someone who shared my same cultural background, norms, as well as someone she could easily speak to in her native tongue, whenever she chooses. Kane was neither bilingual nor Haitian, and I still loved him. My mother's often blanketed prejudiced statements about African-Americans made it seem like she couldn't differentiate between the good individuals and the bad ones. She made it seem as if all the people in her homeland of Haiti were good people, and there were no criminals or bad influences. I was always quick to point out to her the chaos that had been going on in Haiti since the ouster of Jean Claude "Baby Doc" Duvalier in 1986, but that's another story. Bad and good people reside on every corner of this earth. I couldn't blame my mother for being partial to her own culture. That happens with every group of people in the world. Her attitude toward African-Americans made me a little apprehensive about introducing Kane to my family. While my father was more accepting and inviting, however, he was sometimes influenced by my mom's demagoguery whenever he experienced a personal infraction with an African-American. My father thought most black cops, especially acted more racist toward him as a black man sometimes than any other cops, whenever he was pulled over. Most Haitians don't like getting involved with the law, and the biggest shame for them is to be handcuffed by a police officer. My dad was once arrested in Manhattan by a black cop because he had forgotten his wallet at home and couldn't provide his driver's license after being pulled over. The cop didn't even bother to look up his information. His car was impounded and he was arrested. My mother almost had a heart attack that day when my dad called her to post his bail. The case was eventually dismissed by a judge, but the experience left a bad stain in my father's brain. He harbored ill feelings toward African-American cops for a long time.

I wanted my parents to see the goodness in Kane that I saw for myself. I didn't want any preconceived notions on their part, to ruin my chances of building a great relationship with Kane. I didn't want to be forced to make a decision between choosing Kane and my parents. I wanted them all in my life. I wrestled with the idea, as to how to introduce Kane to my family. We were getting serious, and I knew he was an honorable man who wanted to do right by me. Honestly, I was in love with Kane, and I knew he felt the same way. I wasn't going to allow my parents' wrong perception and prejudice toward African-Americans to be a hurdle. I was smart enough to know that Kane was a keeper. Besides, in my Haitian culture, women are not encouraged to date a lot of men. I had only been with one man prior to Kane, and I damn sure didn't have any desire to keep exploring other men sexually, or through casual dating. Kane turned out to be the perfect man for me the second time around. In essence, I got lucky, truly lucky the second time around.

All the gibber about the unprincipled ways of African-Americans coming from my mom, still played a role in my spirit, and was a major factor in my head. I simply wanted my parents to fall in love with Kane's character as much as I did. One of the main reasons I realized that so many immigrants from other countries develop certain prejudices toward African-Americans, is how the mainstream media portrays African-Americans, in order to promote their fake white superiority. In reality, a lot of black people here are no different than other black folks from everywhere else. The media plays a major role dishing out lies and nonfactual stats about black people daily, in addition to portraying us as criminals every chance they get. Juxtaposing the lies they tell about African-Americans and all the lies that they have imparted in the minds of people about Haiti being one of the poorest countries in the western hemisphere, should be enough for people like my mother to understand the mind games these white supremacists play. I had to explain it to my mother in Laymen's terms for her to understand that one of the most common myths about black men that is repeated all the time on television, is that there are more of them in prison than in college. I had to remind her that also applied to my dad, who's her husband, who's a black man in this country. I also made it a point to ask my mother how many black men she personally knew who were in prison. She couldn't even answer the question, because she knew none. This narrative couldn't be further from the truth. There are more black men in college than in prison. However, even some black women have subscribed to this false narrative, whenever they're discussing the topic of the lack of available black men, as it pertains to black romantic relationships. We allow the media to ingrain in our minds false narratives about our own people every day, and in turn, we continue to reinforce their white supremacist garbage against ourselves. It's as if our critical thinking skills are nonexistent, and we now allow the media to feed us whatever bullshit supremacist soup they feel is the appropriate dish for the day. We have to debunk their false narratives and connect the truth to our people and our real struggles. My mother has been my guinea pig, as far as teaching the world the truth about this false white supremacy and savior syndrome that most of these people suffer from.

I had to quickly do the research and show my mom the real facts about black people in this country. She was surprised to learn that the general prison population in the US, which includes all races and genders, is a total of 2.3 million people. "There are over 45 million black people in this country and almost forty-five percent of them are black men. However, these racist people, especially on the Fox News station, like to use analytics that favor white supremacy to hide the fact that over fifty percent of all crimes committed in this country are committed by white people, and over fifty-seven percent of the prison population is white. The breakdown of their analytics goes directly to say that black people are committing more crimes based on the percentage of the black population here. However, black people are also targeted and falsely arrested daily, as was the case with my own father, which I was quick to point out to my mom. It's no different than when former president Ronald Reagan called black women welfare queens, when he knew damn well the majority of welfare recipients in this country were white women at the time, and are still the majority of people on public assistance today. This is fact! The second most popular stereotype is that most black men are absent fathers. That also isn't true. Black men are the most involved fathers in their children's lives in this country. These propaganda and false narratives are sold to the world in order to uphold this fake white supremacy, which is a psychological disorder known as "delusion of grandeur" suffered by most white people. In order for the white race to believe it is supreme, they have to continue to undermine the other races. It's called supremacy under false pretenses. If some of these racists really want to understand supremacy, they just need to take a look at the accomplishments of black people in this country, in spite of all the obstacles, roadblocks, and adversities in their paths, which includes racism that is practiced against black people in all facets of life in America and around the world. There are so many variables as to why some people in the black community are forced into a life of crime, but the most important one is the drug epidemic, which has been brought on by different racist administrations since President Nixon. The racially motivated crusade against black people, which became known as the war on drugs under President Nixon, was the beginning of mass incarceration of most black people as we know it. Reagan would further see the demise of the black community by duplicating Nixon's efforts and multiplying the punishment by ten folds, to ensure the destruction of the black community completely, when thousands of black families suffered the brunt of his strategic attack with the crack epidemic. How can they expect the black community to thrive when the black community is specifically targeted as the center for a crack epidemic, in order to ensure the community's downfall? Anybody with good sense would know and understand that it's difficult for drug-addicted parents to raise children with high morals, values, and principles. Reagan not only started the crack epidemic, but his elixir or antidote was the destructive war on drugs, which led to the incarceration of the people who were recruited to become drug dealers by the CIA, as well as the majority of the drug victims in the black community who lost their livelihood to a covert and orchestrated crack addiction of the people. However, lately, we've seen that the US government has been singing a different tune, as it relates to the meth epidemic in rural America, because the majority of people affected are white. So now, it's no longer a war on drugs, but a crisis and a call to help white families get back on track. Special services and counseling are being provided for these white addicts, instead of a high rate of incarceration for those people selling the meth and the ones who are abusing the meth. Sentences are light, even when white-run meth labs are busted with million dollars worth of meth distribution. Politicians are encouraging counseling centers to be financed by the federal governments all across rural America, in addition to other government subsidiaries to help these white people cope with the meth epidemic around the country. Urban America saw a completely different reaction and tactic to solving the crack epidemic. Black people didn't receive counseling and other services to fight the crack epidemic, because the crack epidemic was specifically designed to destroy the black community."

Educating my mom on the endless marginalization of black people in this country has also been an endless task for me because there's so much to cover. Black people have allowed racist Democratic and Republican administrations to play "Good cop and Bad cop" against them for too long. The two wings are coming from the same bird, and both wings are racist. The camouflaged racist liberals are no better than the overt Republican racists. It was Democratic Senator Joe Biden who introduced the Mass Incarceration legislation, to further uphold Reagan's lofty goal of destroying the black community with a drug epidemic, and it was Bill Clinton who conned the black community into believing he was an honorary brother by appearing on the Arsenio Hall show blowing a saxophone to seal our fate, before he signed that bill into law. Never mind the fact that Hillary Clinton was on national television openly referring to young black men as predators, but black people sealed their own fate by overwhelmingly voting for Bill Clinton. The destruction of the black family was secured, and even the puppets of the Congressional Black Caucus agreed to undermine their own community by voting for that bill. Those same Congressional Black Caucus puppets are now wearing different color glasses and singing a different tune as it pertains to the meth epidemic. Sometimes my mom just sat there and listened without saying anything. I didn't know if she thought I was ranting or not, but my endless soliloquies about black oppression were/are necessary, and I hate that I put my mother through them sometimes, but she has also surprised me many times, by absorbing it all. My mother would have questions after listening to me. She actually paid attention to what I was saying. She cared about my happiness.

"Millions of black children were removed from their homes and placed in foster care as a result of the crack epidemic, because their parents couldn't cope with their personal drug addiction. Millions of crack babies were also produced, due to President Reagan's evil deeds, which has been the underlying factor for the pipeline to prison for so many black boys and men. However, they've also failed to realize that black people don't die, we multiply. No other race or group in the world has demonstrated the resilience of black people. With an array of obstacles, traps, pitfalls, and adversities established to enforce and ensure the demise of black people, the overwhelming majority of us have managed to overcome the odds and succeed, in spite of. I'm certain that white people continue to wonder why black people are not completely decimated yet in this country by their endless inhumane efforts to demoralize and destroy us. With all the privileges afforded to white people in society, why do they still end up committing crimes? We know white criminals are offered due process, and they're only convicted when they're guilty ninety-nine percent of the time. However, black folks are unjustly charged for crimes they don't commit on a regular basis. There are thousands of innocent black people sitting in prison for crimes they never committed. We know that as a fact. The Innocence Project has proven this fact." Of course, these are things that my mom didn't know about the injustice that so many black people face here until her husband was unjustly arrested for committing no crime.

"Furthermore, how come some white people end up living in worst conditions than black people in this country, you probably wonder? The answer to that question is simple; America was founded by a group of criminal thug rejects from England who decided to slaughter the Indians, so they could steal their land, illegally kidnapped Africans to enslave them, so they could build this country for free for their lazy asses, brutally raped and murdered anybody who didn't look like them, and they continue to steal as many resources as possible around the world to maintain this country as a first world society, while simultaneously building debt. Still, some of these white people end up falling victims to their own vices and traps. Their criminal nature is innate, while black people have been forced to compromise their own natural values to survive under their racist system around the entire world." I thought I had said enough, but would you believe it? My mother sat there and listened to my entire diatribe without interrupting me, and then responded with, "I did not know all this bad history about America," she said to me in her thick Haitian accent. "Their tactics are very covert, Mom," I told her. The problem with so many immigrant people is the fact that they place white people on a pedestal before they even arrive here, without understanding most of the time white people are the cause for them fleeing poverty, hunger, instability, and violence in their own country.

Still, for my own sanity, I wish the media would sometimes explain and address certain issues that continue to plague the black community, without using these stereotypes to further marginalize us. They always fail to shed light on the psychological stigma attached to slavery and the trauma that black people have undergone and experienced, not just in this country, but around the world. The Holocaust is acknowledged worldwide, even though it was restricted to Germany. Slavery was global, but all the colonizers refuse to acknowledge its impact and their role in it. One of white people's favorite stigmas about black people they like to latch on to is the absentee father issue that is deeply rooted in slavery, which was forced upon black men by racist slave owners. I didn't want my mother to just hear part of it of this history, because the impact of slavery is broad. I wanted to educate her on all the history she didn't know. I appreciate the fact that my mother was a good listener. "They should talk about how black children were removed from their parents to be enslaved elsewhere, far away from their kin. They must also talk about how strong black men were taken away from their families and sold to other slave exploiters, to become breeders at other plantations. Let's not even talk about the many white men who have raped so many black women and have failed to play the role of father in the lives of their mixed bastard children. That's the origin of the absentee father phenomenon. Despite all that, black men are the most involved in their children's lives in this country. It's very easy for the media to taint the minds of people with propaganda and false narratives that benefit white supremacy while focusing on a specific targeted group of people, in order to protect white privilege and enable white supremacists a platform to spew their false sense of superiority.

Black people have been vilified from the time white people illegally kidnapped them from their homeland in Africa and brought them to the West to establish chattel slavery. The colonization of Africa and the annihilation of the Native Americans in North America and the West Indies took place because these people were well-intentioned and were very welcoming to their European visitors. However, the Europeans were evil people who were bloodthirsty and wanted to exploit the entire world, while using genocide as a favorite tactic. The entire world is late in recognizing and acknowledging the true violent nature of Europeans, their degradation, marginalization, exploitation, and oppression of other people, so they can elevate themselves. In order for a liar to make his lies appear as truths, he must continue to destroy true facts and negatively characterize people and situations in his glorified tales in a way that benefits his own elevated status. White people's nature has not changed, and most of them are thousands of years removed from being civilized. Violence shows lack of ethics and morals. The United States of America and its European allies have tormented the world with violence since the beginning of time. These terrorists just don't know how to stop terrorizing people around the world.

Peace is not part of their trait. Those characteristics are essentially the blueprint of white supremacy, because there's nothing supreme about whiteness. Whiteness is weakness in most cases, which is why these Caucasians continue to create chaos around the world, while presenting themselves as saviors at the same time. That's exactly the tactics that racist white people have used to continue to marginalize, subjugate, oppress, and exploit African-Americans in this country, and black people worldwide. America has never been alone in its racist practices against black people. Racism is practiced all over the world by most European people and European countries against Africans and Caribbean people. As a matter of fact, America was a little bit late to the party. The entire Caribbean had been conquered by their European predecessors before they even got involved in the slave trade." I had to end what I figured my mom thought was a rant, but she surprised me when she asked, "Can you make a list of the books that I should read to learn more about the African-American experience?" I was more than happy to oblige her.

My own parents have often discussed how racism in Haiti, the first free Black Republic in the world, is still rampant. A handful of foreign oligarch families from Europe and the Middle East, in cahoots with America, France, and Canada control the economy and politics in Haiti. All of them are white, or at least some of them think they're white because they're of Arab or Jewish descent. And then there's the wedge these former colonizers created long ago through their illegal raping of black women, between light skinned and dark skinned black people, which gives the mulattoes a false sense of better worth against full-blooded black people in Haiti, and think they deserve better treatment in all black societies across the world, because of the association to the blood of white rapists, most of the time. The colonizers' history of rape dating back to slavery, is well documented, the ancestors in Haiti were not spared the agonizing experience. This hierarchical division was intentionally created by white people to maintain a supreme sense of hierarchy that forces people to believe an ounce of white blood in any person is still better than one hundred percent black blood in a whole human. On the surface, Haiti doesn't appear to be a place where racism exists, but it does to the point where it has corrupted the entire country's government system. The imperialist countries play a major role in positioning these mulattoes in government spaces that can better serve the interest of white supremacy. These foolish delusional Negroes sometimes even try to disassociate themselves with blackness, until they get a dose of reality while traveling overseas when white people see them as nothing more than a regular light-complexioned Negro. The light skin illusion is very pervasive and detrimental to countries across the Caribbean, not just in Haiti.

I realize the failures of African countries and leaders to consolidate their resources to become a united Africa have affected all black countries in the Caribbean, the standard of living for all black people worldwide, and the treatment of black people globally by all other groups of people, but specifically white and Asian people who set out to continue the colonization of Africa and the Caribbean. White imperialists have made sure they set in place parables to fool the entire world, as it relates to white superiority. Having said all of that, which may sound like I went on a tangent to those people who hate to hear the truth, is because I want the world to understand that a lot of black people worldwide are not consciously aware of their functional and psychological deficiencies due to slavery and colonization, which appear to make dysfunction normal to way too many black people. The construct of white supremacy has forced black people to normalize dysfunctions in so many different aspects of our lives, in order to be functional within white society. We are constant actors, because our daily performances to please white people and to function within the systemic racist construct in place have everything to do with our survival. To fool us further, white people have created a system of modern-day slavery, where they are still in control. They normally allow a handful of athletically gifted and talented Negroes to become millionaires and a couple of billionaires, in order to cover their malignant wounds with wealth. It is those millionaire and sometimes billionaire fools that white people can now point to, in order to claim fairness and equality, while they continue to improve on their tactics to marginalize the black masses at large. Unfortunately, black people with money and limited opportunity are too shortsighted to see the bigger picture of how white people use the few to exploit the many. These black millionaires often become the mouthpieces and gatekeepers for the racists who want to build upon a system of exploitation, marginalization, and subjugation by using the black voice and black people to normalize their racist practices. The indoctrination of black people is reinforced daily on the news, because most of the anchors talking negatively about black people on the news are black themselves. For now, I'm gonna leave it there, before I offend a few people who believe that all black stories should be for entertainment purposes and a distraction from their daily lives, even though the exploitation of black people is part of their daily lives. We all should be aware of our own marginalization, and our exploitation should never be relegated to complaints.

My father was the open-minded one between my parents, and the person who treated me like I could do no wrong, ever since I was a baby. I knew that I had to appease him, so he could understand the love that I had for Kane. In many ways, my father bred in me the love that I developed for Kane. The love manifested itself when I started to take inventory of Kane's demeanor, characteristics and compared how he and my dad treated me in the same special way. Though Kane's approach and love was a little different because we were in an amorous relationship, however, he prioritized my needs the same way my daddy always does. Kane always makes me feel special in both his presence, or while I'm away from him. It was normal for him to send me random texts to let me know he was thinking about me, or how I brought so much joy to his life. Of course, I reciprocated as well, but his gestures are not the norm for men, according to what I've heard from other women. The only other person to have ever made me feel so special all the time is my daddy. I knew once my dad was on board with the relationship, my mother would come along as well, in due time. The few times that I traveled home to New York to visit my parents, I decided to start buttering up my dad before I introduced my parents to Kane. When I say buttering him up, I meant I was slowly spoon-feeding him the random good qualities I would look for in a guy, regardless of his ethnic background. I primarily focused on morals, principles, and values that were similar to my dad's. I also worked on my daddy and his views of African-Americans for months, in order to strip his mind of any prejudices, before I decided to bring Kane home to meet my family, without ever mentioning to them that I was dating Kane. Haitian parents are a little different when it comes to their daughters dating. The boys have free will to do whatever they want to do, but the girls are monitored and scrutinized with very little liberty to even go out on dates. My dad was the typical Haitian father in that way. I didn't have to test him, because I already knew. However, I also love the fact that my dad is a learner. He has never acted like he knew everything about anything, but he would school me whenever he became knowledgeable enough about something, or anything. He would hear me out whenever I gave him information that he wasn't privy to about people, places, events, inventions, situations, or anything that could be enlightening to him. Inquisitive is an understatement, as it relates to my dad's thirst for knowledge. I had to make my father understand the hardship that African-Americans faced here as a marginalized group in this country, and the struggle and hurdles they've had to overcome, so that other black immigrants like himself could even be allowed to move to this country and enjoy the benefits of half decent human rights that African-Americans are continuously fighting for. The fight seems endless, though, and it's going to take the entire black Diaspora to fight for the changes needed to eradicate the racist system that continues to oppress black folks here. Black immigrants need to band together with their fellow African-American brethren to form a united front to overcome racism, not just in America, but across the world.

The African-American voice is one of the strongest voices that black people have around the world, and it's also the most influential culturally, thanks to Hip Hop, R & B, Jazz, boxing, the NBA, and the NFL. The high visibility of influential people like Michael Jordan, LeBron James, Kobe, P-Diddy, Kanye West, and many others should be used as an asset to change the world for black people all over. We can't just allow these people to become culture vultures who can dictate what position the high profile black people should take on issues. These black folks should not be restricted to the roles of entertainers and athletes. Whether they like it or not, their voices are stronger than the black populace. They are revered by people all over the world, and there's strength in that position they should and must use to change the situation for black people all over the world.

Through my limited travels to a few countries around the world, I couldn't help but notice that black people are marginalized everywhere. There's a domino effect worldwide, whenever black people fight against injustice. What happens in South Africa can affect black people in America. What black people fight against in America can also affect South Africa. The sooner we realize the potential of our unification to fight issues globally, the better off we will be as a race. Most black immigrants who just arrived in America are just enjoying the benefits of the struggles that African-Americans went through without merit. Black immigrants must earn meritocracy. I talk to my parents about that all the time. My father gets it, most of the time, but my mom is a little more difficult to let go of her stubbornness. She tends to believe that a lot of black people are in their unfortunate positions in this country, because they want to be. She's blinded by the limited opportunities afforded black people here, which forces her to also turn a blind eye to systemic racism. My job is to try my best to educate her, because although I'm her Haitian-American daughter, I'm primarily seen as an African-American woman in society. African-Americans have been fighting oppression for over four hundred years in this country, and each time they have started to make strides, the racist system gets more innovative with its approach to continue its marginalization of them. Because of my dad, I've always understood that education is the key to understanding everything in life. I made it my business to always educate him. I had to let my dad know that most immigrants, not just black ones, usually end up sharing the resources of the African-American community when they first arrive here, because most immigrants tend to move to the black community to get their lives started here because the black community is welcoming to almost everyone. When I say black community, I'm also including the Caribbean community, because Caribbean folks usually live in close proximity to the African-Americans. It is usually after these immigrants have established themselves after being here for several years that many of them tend to seek refuge in the white suburbs. Most of the sub-communities, like the Hispanics, Indians, and Africans, are also near or share proximity with the African-American communities here. While the Flatbush area in Brooklyn has a strong Caribbean presence, it is close in proximity to Brownsville and other African-American communities, and even before the West Indian people arrived to Brooklyn, Flatbush was mostly an African-American community. However, they've allowed the Caribbean people to make the transition and assimilation to create their own community and establish their own culture within

Flatbush and among African-Americans. We have to acknowledge those facts.

My father had heard of Dr. Martin Luther King while growing up in Haiti, because there's a street in Haiti named in honor of Dr. Martin Luther King, but he never really delved into the Civil Rights Movement. I had to bring home many books from the library to educate my father on the scope of the Civil Rights Movement, and the other black heroes like Frederick Douglas, Harriet Tubman, Dr. W.E. B. Dubois, Marcus Garvey, and many more who had fought to make things better for black people in America. We still have a long way to go, but these people sacrificed their livelihood for the betterment of all black people in this country. I also made my father aware of the fact that West Indians have also played a major role in advancing black folks in this country. When Jean Baptist Point Du Sable, a Haitian merchant, first discovered Chicago, who do you think were moving to Chicago first? Of course, it was black people. Malcolm X's father was West Indian, W.E.B. Dubois has Haitian roots, and Minister Louis Farrakhan's family originated from Trinidad. The cultures definitely crossed in the fight for justice here, but they were united then. In the process of learning about the Civil Rights Movement and Dr. King, my dad also discovered Malcolm X, W.E.B. Dubois and he became a fan of these people right away. While he respects Dr. King's determination, vision, zeal, and drive to convince white people we were their equal and to allow us to live among them, my dad became more a fan and follower of the teachings of Malcolm X. He wanted nothing to do with desegregation, because he came from a Noiriste society where black people were encouraged to thrive. After all, the land from which he came is the most rebellious and full of revolutionaries. My mother on the hand, though stubborn, never disagreed with my dad for too long, because my dad had his own way of getting through to her, and he could always make her see the reasoning in everything. My mother's just a different breed. She simply wants to live her life and mind her own business. She tends to see things differently with more of a closed mind because of her upbringing, but my dad's methods seem to always work perfectly for her, which is why they mesh.

I would recommend that all black immigrants who migrate to this country become very familiar with the injustices that black people have faced here since slavery and familiarize themselves with the black struggles and fights that make it possible for them to enjoy certain rights as African descent people when they arrive in America. I understand that most immigrants who move here often think that America is the land of milk and honey, so they tend to place white people on a pedestal, without realizing the milk and honey they find in America sometimes come from the sweat and tears of their own ancestors in their homeland, which is stolen by the US government, as well as the free labor of the African-American ancestors who helped build this strong, rich and most developed country that America has managed to become around the world. The ancestors who spent their entire lives working for free and those who died on the cotton fields deserve a lot of credit for the construction of America and America's self-proclamation as the leader of the world.

A nation can only prosper economically when they have the natural resources and the labor force to maximize its production. White America lacked the labor force, the manpower, the ingenuity, the work ethic, and the physical ability from its inception, to build this country into a first world, which is why they went to Africa and illegally and forcibly kidnapped Africans, use treachery, religion, and the bible to convince them their souls needed to be cleansed and forced them into slavery. We also know that North America still lacks the natural resources for this country to compete against the rest of the world, so every country with resources has become prey to their predatory approach of international trade, especially countries that lack the military might to stand up to America.

I realize too often people can never see a thief coming, it's only after they realized their possessions have been stolen that most people understand that they were in the company of a thief. There's no such thing as a wolf in sheep's clothing. A wolf acts and growls completely differently than a sheep, but a lot of folks don't want to take the time to acknowledge the wolf's demeanor, behavior, and history. Well, the US government is that thief. They play hero, savior, manipulator, oppressor, and exploiter all at the same time. There's nothing sheepish about them. We know who they are. However, a lot of black immigrants try to act oblivious to the racist tactics and practices that all the colonizing nations have forced upon them. They want to escape poverty that is implemented against them in their own country by puppets chosen by those same colonizers they glorify. In order to get a visa to the United States and other European nations that have been built off the sweat of Africans, they usually forgo their own logic and are usually caught up with the false ideals of an American dream or European dream by overworking, while being underpaid, exploited, because they have been fooled to believe that's the way to achieve their dream. It's reminiscent of the hard-working field slaves being rewarded with chitlins (chitterlings), also known as pig intestines, as an edible part of the pig for a meal during slavery after working in the hot sun all day, because it was better to clean pig feces to eat it, instead of going hungry. Imagine convincing yourself that eating the intestines of pigs is a better option than not eating anything at all? This logic may be difficult for some people to swallow, but the racist tactics that are practiced in America, are also practiced throughout Africa, the Caribbean, and other regions of the world that are inhabited by people of color.

A lot of black immigrants don't want to understand white racism, especially if they moved to this country illegally. They usually have no choice but to be submissive, passive, subservient, and docile to the racist system, in order to avoid any confrontation with the law, which might lead to their deportation for the most insignificant infraction. Their survival is dependent upon submission. Even legal immigrants have to bow down to white supremacy and racists, because the immigration laws still threaten their livelihood on a daily basis, and protects white privilege at all times. They cannot afford to commit the most petty of crimes or be acquainted with the judicial system in any way, because deportation looms at the first felony offense. We are already aware of the insurmountable number of black people who are serving prison time because they have been set up by filthy racist cops. This fear of deportation was reinforced after Barrack Obama was elected president. As the first elected black president of this country, Obama introduced legislation that made it even easier for black immigrants to be deported back to their homeland for the smallest infraction, and sometimes even American-born citizens were erroneously deported, just because they have a foreign last name. As a matter of fact, Obama was called "The Deporter In Chief" because so many people of color were deported under his administration. It almost seemed as if Obama was specifically targeting people of color. He refused to address reparations for black people as president, while at the same time, he was signing reparation checks to the Jewish community for a holocaust that took place in Germany and across some other countries in Europe.

President Obama was probably the worse puppet that the entire continent of Africa and the Caribbean had seen. His policies further impoverished Africa and the Caribbean, while he strengthened the presence of the United States in those regions. It was under the Obama administration that the government of Ghana agreed to have the United States install a military base to monitor growth in Ghana. Furthermore, symbolically, Obama should have made it a priority as the first black president to take a trip to Haiti, because Haiti was the first black country that liberated itself from slavery. Haiti was also the reason the United States expanded its territories exponentially. France lacked the resources to go to war with the US at the time because they had been fighting the Haitians, which forced them to sell their territories to the United States for a fraction of what they were worth. It's not a coincidence that Obama never took a trip to Haiti. He was also responsible for installing a former crackhead musician and puppet to help squander some of Haiti's natural resources. If he didn't care about the livelihood of African-Americans as president, why would he care about the livelihood of Haitians?

Obama acted like the black holocaust was not specific to the United States during his two-term presidency, because this country was the only country in North America to import slaves onto its soil for free labor. The other European colonizer practiced slavery from a distance. They established territories in Africa, the Caribbean, and South America that produced enough goods to turn their resource-challenged and barren countries in Europe into fully developed and economically sustainable first world paradise for white people, while the Africans they enslaved lived in hell. That didn't matter to President Obama, though. The Jewish holocaust continues to take precedence to the sufferings of Africans, a suffrage that took place all across the world, but not even the first black president of this country bothered to acknowledge that black people here and all over the world, whose ancestors had been enslaved, deserve reparations for the wrongs imposed against them. President Obama himself is the son of an African immigrant. His father was from Kenya. How ironic? When it comes to immigration rules and guidelines for black people in America, there's always more than meets the eye. It's not as easy or clear as people perceive. We already know that most African-Americans have to work twice as hard to get ahead here as citizens of this nation, even those with undeniable natural talent, but many of them also have no idea how much harder it can be for black and brown immigrants who have to assimilate into a new culture, learn a new language and customs that is foreign to them, and really have very little choice in their displacement from their homeland, in order to survive. As a former attorney, senator, and politician, I'm sure Obama is also an historian who is fully aware of the fact that Haitian soldiers assisted the United States in their fight against the British during the revolutionary war in 1775.

Our complexion may be the same as our identifier as black people, but black immigrants have their own cultural norms that they sometime bring here with them, but they are also subjected to the same maltreatment as African-Americans by white people, because white people can't generally differentiate the different cultures. These are all variables that most of them are not familiar with, or have ever experienced in their own countries. Sometimes black immigrants receive more flack from their own African-American brethrens, because of language barriers and cultural differences before assimilation takes place. Unfortunately, some African-Americans are foolish enough to believe the US government automatically offers aid and other financial assistance to black immigrants when they first arrive in America. That couldn't be further from the truth. This falsehood has created animosity toward black immigrants from African- Americans because they have been fighting for reparations since slavery ended. That kind of animosity affects commonsense, and creates further division among black people. Imagine a racist country that refuses to take care of its own black citizens, giving handouts to black immigrants? That shit would only make sense in the minds of the indoctrinated, ignorant, and confused. The US government does no such thing to help black immigrants. I know all of this, because I've lived it and seen the struggles my parents have faced since they've been in this country.

The system in place in America is designed to protect white privilege and promote white supremacy at all costs, which means that white immigrants are more likely to receive some form of aid when they first arrive here, just like they received free land over black people who had been here centuries before they came. One of the main reasons racist white people are quick to yell out to black people, "Go back to Africa!" is because this racist system established by the US government long ago has always reassured white people of their rights as true Americans, even those who migrated here, while treating black people as adopted Americans, hence the reason they refer to black people in this country as African-Americans. In the same way that white immigrants strengthen white supremacy when they arrive here, black people should focus more on the contribution of black immigrants to their group in this country, and embrace their presence, which strengthens the black community overall. I'm certain when the Haitian merchant, Jean Baptiste Point Du Sable discovered Chicago he was not extending an olive branch to white folks for them to move to Chicago. His discovery was about settling in a place that was comfortable for his black family and people. The division hadn't come into play yet.

We shouldn't just require African-Americans to have a better understanding of the complexities of black division in this country, in order to establish better relationships with black immigrants, but the black immigrants also need to respect the existence, struggles, and fight of the African-Americans when they move to America.

The complexities of racism and white supremacy require a higher level of intelligence, understanding, and education, in order to decipher all the schemes and scams within the system. Unfortunately, the majority of black immigrants who migrate to America get so caught up with working two, and sometimes three jobs, to make ends meet and to help their family back home, the only thing they have time to decipher is their survival in a new culture, new environment, and new world. In addition to getting assimilated to new customs and traditions, oftentimes they also have to learn a new language, if they didn't come from an English-speaking country, which adds to the difficulties of understanding racist US policies, as it concerns African-Americans and even themselves. In the same breath, the majority of African-Americans are also caught up with their own survival here, so they don't have time to decipher the immigration policies, as it relates to black immigrants in this country. Most immigrants who live here don't even know the reason behind the big Thanksgiving celebration in this country every year, but almost all of them celebrate and participate in it, because it's about familiarizing themselves with American customs and traditions, so they can fit in. Most immigrants accept that Thanksgiving is about family togetherness, and the history behind it doesn't even matter to most of them. That's the part of white supremacy that makes most black people living in America completely dysfunctional due to lack of awareness of true white history. However, most black people have learned to function within this dysfunctional system that they fight hard for and against every day in order to be a respectable member of American society. The celebration of the annihilation of Native Americans every fourth Thursday in November of every year is business as usual. Most black people, whether Immigrants or African-Americans, see nothing wrong with celebrating many of the US holidays. Nobody takes the time to understand the power of white supremacy and the falsehoods that it encompasses. That is the part of white supremacy we should be most concerned about. They have normalized so many of their own dysfunctions for us, sometimes we find ourselves defending their atrocities, in order to prove our patriotism. Some of these holidays should be abolished. However, they have made zombies out of all of us, because we all want to assimilate into a culture that forces black people to prove their allegiance to a country that has only accepted black people for their labor contribution, athletic prowess, and resilience to allow their constant persecution of us while we resist revolting.

We live in the most dysfunctional country in the world, and my parents walked right into that fire when they emigrated here from Haiti. If we can set aside our differences and focus on the fact that we need to unite as a group of Africans, their marginalization of us wouldn't be so effective, not in America, or anywhere in the world. White people have mastered the art of unification to destroy us all over the world, while we continue to struggle to unite and destroy ourselves in the process. I had to learn all this history through my own research because no one made me aware of the true history of this country. My dad also influenced my thirst for knowledge. Meeting Kane gave me an entirely different perspective on black life in America. I wanted to know about the struggles of his ancestors, his strife, and all the adversities and obstacles that he has to deal with as a black man in America. When I heard about my dad's struggles from Haiti to here, it opened my eyes to many different things. After all, I was about to create a family with this man, and his lineage would be represented in my children. I have to be aware of his entire family's history and struggles.

I was excited about introducing Kane to my family. I really, with all my heart, wanted my family to embrace him completely. I didn't know if I was ready to choose love over my family if I had to, but I was hoping it didn't have to come to that. While I was worried about my family embracing my wonderful boyfriend, I didn't really give much thought to Kane's family accepting me. I knew there might be some prejudices because of our different cultural backgrounds, but not anything that would be relevant enough to break us up. I didn't lose sleep over it. For some reason, I have always thought of African-Americans as more accepting than their fellow Caribbean and African people. African-Americans have had to learn to share their resources and communities with most of the newly arrived black immigrants who move to America. Many African-Americans in the black community usually don't make a fuss about sharing their resources with others, because black folks in general are communal in nature. We tend to look out for one another, even when there's a language barrier and cultural differences. It's a conflict because ignorance still festers at times. Of course, there's an exception to every rule. Occasionally, some immigrants would run into an ignorant African-American who would tell them to go back to their country, but that behavior is learned and rooted in the racism that they experience at the hands of white people here daily. That mindset and attitude came from the white people who oppress and marginalize them in every way. It's very common for racist white people to tell black people who have helped build this country to go back to Africa, whenever they get into a disagreement with an African-American, or just want to spew their hatred toward black people, as if they have receipts for the goods this country stole from Africa. The basis of this ire originated from white people's nature to control and dominate everything in totality, including people and other countries' resources around the world, even though they continuously preach self-reliance, independence, and sufficiency.

First, we must remember that they kidnapped and brought most black people here in chains, and against their will. I have never in my life seen anybody try to return illegally-gotten stolen goods back to a store. Telling someone to "Go back to Africa, or wherever," is always the easiest insult they can spew, as if the Native Americans don't have the right to tell them to take their asses back to

Europe. People living on stolen land are often blinded by their own theft, so they subconsciously project their own insecurities onto other people. Still, a lot of black folks aren't conscious enough of the bad habits they've picked up from white people through their assimilation process, into a culture that was forced upon them, which was also foreign to their ancestors when they got here. We better understand quickly that we cannot afford to pick up their bad habits. For the most part, our nature has remained intact, because we are a welcoming people naturally.

Over the course of their assimilation into American culture, a lot of black people from the Caribbean and Africa usually experience this rude awakening in the most difficult way that they are more connected to their African-American brethrens than the people who set out to marginalize all of us. In the end, many black immigrants end up realizing that they have to adopt the mindset of African-Americans, as it relates to racism for their own survival in America, because racism doesn't differentiate between the different black subcultures anywhere in this racist country, or anywhere in the world, for that matter. We all suffer the same fate at the hands of the racist system in place worldwide. All black people have their blackness and African ancestry in common in the face of white imperialism. In addition, the racist system in place is stabilized, as long as they continue to approach us as a monolith, regardless of our differences. Most of the time, they can't or don't even care to differentiate between the different subgroups of black people, because racism is limited to our skin color, not our accents, achievements, individuality, or uniqueness. However, it is a greater disservice to black people when we continue to differentiate every little thing among ourselves, to maintain this division that benefits the racist system in place. We should encourage one another to acknowledge and embrace the myriad of flavors within all of our cultures in the African Diaspora, and we must not hold our differences as true evidence to become strangers, enemies, and foes who continue to empower white supremacy by employing division. The oppressors' assessment of our existence is often limited to prejudice and racism against us and our skin color, which is the main reason why we must always unite under the umbrella of our blackness. It's not to say that a person is letting go of their own culture, but we should not be opposed to celebrating all black cultures. Do you know how weird it is to see a black person celebrating Saint Patrick's Day? A lot of black people do it, nonetheless, while they have a harder time celebrating other black cultures. We should make it our duty to educate our children and inspire them to celebrate the different variations of black cultures around the world.

From my perspective, it seems that Black adult immigrants usually endure less problems dealing with assimilation into American life, because they tend to be less enthusiastic about acceptance, and less preoccupied with assimilating into American society. Adult immigrants tend to embrace their own culture a lot more, and they always try to stay relevantly close to their homeland's culture when they first arrive here. More often, they are also focused on work and opportunities, and have more patience and tolerance for racist bullshit, because their goal is to strive for a better life at all costs. I say this, because I saw how my own parents navigated this racist world while growing up. My parents have always been focused and determined, especially my mom. My dad is more observant, so he pays closer attention to white people's nature, behavior, and their zeal to be super incumbent in their dominant space in the world, as it relates to other races, but especially the black race. Not to say that all immigrants have tendencies to be more subservient, docile, and submissive to white people when they get here, but oftentimes, they have no choice because of problems with their legal status when they first arrive in America. Their exposure to ignorance is also limited, because they normally travel straight from home to work, work to home, or the supermarket and other pertinent places only while running errands. I know that my own mother very seldom socialize with anybody who doesn't share her Haitian heritage. I'm not sure if it's a defense mechanism or a sense of comfort and belonging around her own people, but she avoids interacting with other people as much as possible. There's also a lack of trust, because she feels American behavior is unpredictable. However, for a person like myself who was born and raised here as a child, the experience is different. Most children like myself, want to socialize and be accepted by their peers, and the African-American kids sometimes teased me and the other foreign black kids in my community when they first arrive here, just because our cultural norms are different. Even though I was born in Brooklyn, it doesn't mean I wasn't teased because of the way my parents dressed me and some of the other cultural norms I've purported publicly.

Most Haitian parents don't prioritize fashion and brand names, simply because they can't afford it. They pay very little attention to brand names, as it relates to fashion, and to be honest, they don't care, because they're more focused on pulling their family out of poverty. Every time you see a Haitian immigrant living in a foreign country, that immigrant is more than likely responsible for an entire village of people. They leave their own country not just to seek a better life for themselves, but also for all the people they left behind who rely on them as a provider. It's a cultural norm that most people won't understand, but it's also part of the responsibility of being Haitian. Most of the time, Haitian parents won't spend extravagant amounts of money on brand-name clothing and shoes for their children, and for that, many Haitian children are teased at school. For the most part, Haitian immigrant parents are mostly occupied with earning a living and providing a better life for their family in this country and those left behind in their home country. They left their country for better opportunities, and they want to maximize those opportunities. The latest fashion is not even on their list of priority. American society is consumed by fashion and other frivolous and trivial nonsense. At the end of the day, fashion only encourages consumerism. We don't even pay attention to the fact that fashion is recycled. Fashion is almost like medicine, where doctors continue to prescribe medication to ease pain and provide temporary relief, without curing anything. Fashion is cyclical, and the fashion industry relies on the addiction of people to consumerism to sustain that industry. Clothing should be timeless, but we're conditioned to believe our sense of style has to match the population at large. I understand innovation as well, but we should not be indebted to an industry that creates arrogant, pompous assholes who think their creativity puts them above the rest of us. We don't need a particular brand of clothing to function or survive in this world, but American capitalism has forced this false sense of consumerism on all of us; and when we are not wearing certain brands, they want to make us feel worthless. Generally, poor people wear expensive items they can't afford to cover their personal shortcomings. It's just a band-aid covering a wound created long ago by white supremacy, when our ancestors were made to feel worthless.

We must also acknowledge the fact that kids usually want to spend time with their peers and be accepted by them, even when they have their differences. The different cultural norms should lead to dialogue instead of disagreements, but too often we find more reasons to divide ourselves than to unite as black people. It starts in the home with the proper home training and education from the black parents, because ignorant children usually grow up to become ignorant adults. Everything about our behavior is rooted in slavery. They shifted our behavior and nature to their own after they kidnapped our forefathers and force them onto those slave ships.

The fact that most immigrant children almost never wear brand-name clothing, usually leads to African-American children teasing us at school or the playground. I was one of those kids being teased all the time for the way that I dressed. It's not as if my parents dressed me funny or anything, but they didn't mind buying me clothes at Walmart. As a kid, I didn't care what type of clothing I wore. I always felt great in my new outfits, but that's not how my peers saw it. Then again, kids always find reasons to tease one another anyway. It's just part of the growing pains, but black immigrant children sometimes allow themselves to be scarred for life by the treatment they receive at the hands of their African-American peers and their consumer culture, without understanding that the oppressed in this country are forced to stay in the position where their dignity lies in what they can hardly afford to buy and wear on their bodies. Those were my problems as a youth, but I managed through them. I don't recall my parents ever having any issues with any of their African-American neighbors. They were always cordial and respectful to us, and as we were with them.

HAITI:

EYE-OPENING
EXPERIENCE

I recognized very early in life that I was growing up in an American society that is preoccupied with excess, capitalism and consumerism, whereas my Haitian immigrant parents came from a place where an overwhelming majority of people are only able to consume the daily basic necessities with few excesses. Just like any other society in the world, Haiti also has its "one percent" ruling class that is primarily made up of greedy white and mulatto predators, who continue to have a monopoly on every business entity and enterprises in Haiti. My parents took me to Haiti for the first time when I was twelve years old, to visit their place of origin and birth. I was ecstatic about visiting a new place that was different from the country that I lived in all my life, and to connect with my place of lineage. The euphoria I felt the night before we left was like nothing I had ever felt before. I couldn't wait to be in a place where people didn't frown upon me because of the way I look. However, when my parents were packing their suitcases, I wondered why they were bringing 4 suitcases full of clothing and other items for a trip that was supposed to last 2 weeks. I didn't question it, I just accepted it. Even the trip to the airport was exciting to me, because I had never been to an airport. The next day, we woke up very early and called a cab to take us to the airport. I was shocked all those huge suitcases fit in the trunk of the cab, but he got us there in no time. While boarding the plane, I was shocked to see so many white people were on the plane going to Haiti for whatever reason. As far as I knew, Haiti was not a popular tourist destination at the time, as there was unrest in the country because of the ouster of the president. Still, there were plenty of white exploiters, I mean explorers, on the plane on their way down to Haiti to explore God knows what about the country's natural resources. My curiosity got the best of me while I was sitting there between my parents. "Dad, why are there so many white people on the plane on their way to Haiti?" I turned to my father and asked. He looked me straight in the eyes and lowered his voice to say, "A lot of Haitians don't know that Haiti is full of minerals and other resources that the world needs. These people are probably on their way to Haiti to rape the country economically." My dad was very blunt. "What does that mean?" I asked, because I didn't understand his lingo at the time. "I can't fully explain in detail right now, because you're too young to understand the history of Haiti, but in due time, I will teach you about Haiti, so you can understand the popular narrative being shared by the media about Haiti being the poorest country in the Western hemisphere, is only used as a veil, in order for these racist exploiters to squander the country's resources. The Haitian people are poor, because of Western imperialism. They have seen to it that Haiti stays in a state of devastation, so that Haiti's rich history of defeating white supremacy can be aligned with their false racist narratives about black people not being able to govern themselves worldwide," my dad said. I always anticipated a history lesson from Dad, and he has never failed to deliver. I started giving the white people on the plane the side eye. I wasn't falling for their fake smiles and false sense of heroism. Most of them were acting like they were missionaries on the way to Haiti to save poor Haitian kids. I started to eavesdrop on their conversation, and many of them were bragging about their missionary work in Haiti, their NGO's and how they were dedicated to help pull the poor people of Haiti out of their misery.

Unfortunately, a lot of the people in Haiti didn't know any better, because these people were on their way to Haiti to improve their own lifestyles financially. Every time these people landed in Haiti, they were there to increase the misery, devastation, and destitution, while enriching themselves. These impostors used religion as a front to gain access to the country. Historically, America, France, Canada, and the rest of these European imperialists, have never been friends of Haiti. They are the biggest foes of the first Free Black Republic in the world.

I can say visiting Haiti was life-altering, overly shocking, and transformative for me, since I had grown up around a lot of Haitians in the Flatbush section of Brooklyn where my parents lived, before we moved to Queens. Most Haitians I've encountered in America pretend they were well-off when they lived in Haiti. They often brag about having maids and other servants, without realizing they are mentally enslaved and reinforcing slavery in a different way at the same time, because the servants are usually underpaid and treated inhumanely by most people who hire them. In addition, a lot of Haitians have normalized "Restaveks" in Haiti, which is essentially the abuse of children who are often given as a trade-off to families who promise to provide them with room and board and a proper education. More often than not, these children end up getting abused by the families who make false promises to their parents. They end up being errand boys and girls for the family, and they never see a day of formal schooling. Their maltreatment around the country is a well-known and open secret. The Haitian government offers no protection for these abused children who sometimes have been orphaned, because of many different circumstances, and have no choice but to become a "Restavek." These children sometimes can be as young as eight years old and expected to have adult duties, such as walking long distances to fetch water. They often have to carry big buckets of water on their heads, when the water is shut off at the residence. They sometimes have to sweep the yard, run to the local market for grocery shopping, and perform other duties that the families' children wouldn't perform. It is a form of accepted modern slavery in Haiti that needs to be eradicated. Slavery by any other name is just a lie. I was able to witness this practice firsthand, when my parents were pointing to the many adults in my mother's neighborhood in Port-Au-Prince who were known as former "Restaveks" as children before my parents left Haiti.

My heart ached for them, and I couldn't understand how some people could be so cruel to children. This "Restavek" practice is also rooted in slavery. We can still look at archived pictures of white people resting their feet on the backs of black children while sitting down as if they're step stools. There are also pictures of them being carried around on the backs of black people and other denigrating and oppressive practices by white people. A lot of the children who fall victim to the practice of "Restavek" are often from the rural parts of Haiti, and their parents sometimes volunteer them to this abhorrent and shameful cultural norm. Most of the customs that black people still practice against their own people today is learned behavior they were exposed to by white people.

It was great to see and enjoy the camaraderie among the people in my father's provincial town of St. Marc, where I saw people living with the basic necessities and looking happy and stress-free in the process. It was a different story when I visited my mother's family in the capital city of Port-Au-Prince. St. Marc is about an hour's drive away from the capital, but the two places seemed like worlds apart. The people in St. Marc were very cordial and pleasant to be around. No one walked by another person without greeting "good morning, good afternoon," or whatever the appropriate greeting of the day happened to be. Everything looked pristine and green.

My father was embraced by the entire community everywhere we went, and everybody was happy to see him, and felt overjoyed by his presence. Some of the neighbors even brought fruits and vegetables to my grandmother's house for them. At first, it didn't make sense to me that people with so very little were willing to share what they had with a man who had left his town years ago for a better life. In return, my dad was also generous with the neighbors. It was then that I realized why my parents brought so many suitcases with them to Haiti. My dad brought different gift items for everyone he remembered in his neighborhood, and he gave money to a few of the neighbors. Everyone seemed to be appreciative of the gifts they received from my father, no matter how big or small it was. This was a different experience for me. I had never been exposed to an actual village or village life, but my father was raised by the village. The communal sense of the people of St. Marc made me wonder why Haiti is not a stronger nation. I saw unity and black people without much, working together and being completely cordial for the first time in my life. I'm not saying that I witnessed total bliss and complete harmony among the Haitian people everywhere that I went, but in most of the villages that my father took me to, so he could introduce me to his family and friends, I saw nothing but harmony, joy, and peace. I want to be clear about that. I could see that folks in the rural parts of Haiti were a lot more friendly, receptive, and kinder to strangers and the people they knew, which was totally different from what I experienced in the United States. I also noticed why people couldn't afford to be wasteful in Haiti, which was where the great habits of my parents originated from, and they've continued to maintain these miserly habits to this day, even after they had been living in the United States for almost two decades. They also taught me not to be wasteful in any way. I appreciate them for that every day. I want to pass those lessons on to my children.

My parents have never forgotten their humble beginnings, and they've reared me with those same morals and principles of hard work, determination and to conserve my hard-earned money for better things and a better future for my children. While my mom's family was considered upper middle class in Haiti, their middle-class status didn't carry much weight financially. It's not like they had hundreds of thousands of dollars at their disposal. They earned just enough money to stay above the fray of poverty in Haiti and to provide a better future for their child. My grandparents owned a business that kept them afloat financially, but I wouldn't call them middle class per se. In comparison to St. Marc, Port-Au-Prince seemed like a zoo to me. My grandparents lived in the suburbs of "Canape Vert," which I was told by my parents used to be one of the most upscale and quietest neighborhoods in Port-Au-Prince. It didn't appear to be that way anymore when I visited Haiti. My mom had plenty of stories about walking the streets safely without a care, and how few people were strangers to her, because most of the people surrounding her had been in the neighborhood since she was born. During our tour around my mother's old neighborhood, the only question that my mother could ask my grandparents about the neighborhood was, "What happened?" The decay of the community was obvious, as her street was filled with dilapidated homes, potholes, and trash littered the roads. Street vendors were everywhere trying to make a dollar out of fifteen cents to survive, selling almost anything and everything that people were willing to pay a little money for. The drive through Port-Au-Prince was hellish and scary. It seemed as if no one respected the traffic laws or rules, and the rudeness of those people in Port-Au-Prince was overbearing. There were hardly any traffic lights, so caution was thrown to the wind. It was every man for himself, and the fastest and most fearless man had the right of way. I can never complain about traffic in Atlanta or anywhere in the United States after what I experienced as a child in Haiti. It took us half a day to travel about 15 miles from my father's hometown to my grandparents' house in Canape Vert. Port-Au-Prince was definitely the most overpopulated and chaotic city that I have ever visited to this day. I can't say there was any present danger, because my parents didn't seem to fear the interaction with other people. My parents tried their best to explain the situation in Port-Au-Prince, as I had many questions.

The obvious chaos with traffic was one of the main reasons I became inquisitive about life in Haiti. However, when my parents decided to go to "Marche Salomon," because of a type of nostalgia, for having not been there for so long, I wondered if all the vendors at the market were able to make a living coming to the market every day to sell their goods. My dad had a very pragmatic explanation for the chaos. He explained that most of the farmers or planters, would bring their goods to the city from the countryside, very early in the morning, and they would set up shop and service their regular customers early, so by the end of the day anything that they sell would be additional profits. It seemed like a tug of war, because the street vendors were right up in parents' faces trying to convince them to come to their stands, while they were negotiating prices with another vendor. By the time we left the market, I felt exhausted, but I still wanted to know why there were so many people in Port-Au-Prince. This particular question was easier for my dad to respond to, because he was born and raised in St. Marc, but had come to Port-Au-Prince to study.

My mom spent her entire life in the capital city, so the contrast would've been a little harder for her to explain. With curiosity in my eyes, as I stared through my parents waiting for an explanation for the chaos, my dad turned to me and said, "Baby girl, Port-Au-Prince is like any other major city in any country or state. A lot of people tend to believe there are more opportunities in the city than in the country or rural areas, so people move to the city to explore those opportunities. In the case of Haiti, unfortunately, a lot of the people who move to the city aren't necessarily skilled to be in the city, but they don't like being in the country, because Haitians look down on country people, but especially farmers, or planters as they are known in Haiti." It wasn't something I understood right away, so I formulated my thoughts before I hit my dad with a follow-up question. "If they're not skilled enough to be here, why are they here? Also, what's wrong with farmers?" My dad could sense my naiveté, so he looked at me, smiled, and said, "There's absolutely nothing wrong with farmers, but when folks are not educated enough to understand the value of agriculture to an economy, they devalue the most precious group of contributors to their economy. Farmers are looked down upon in Haiti because most Haitians prefer foreign goods over their own national goods, which is one of the reasons why the Haitian economy has been in freefall for so long." My dad never spoken down to me like I was an intellectually underdeveloped child. He understood that I was mentally keen enough to engage intellectually on a level that most teenagers my age couldn't fathom at the time. I wasn't ready for a lesson in economy, but I was definitely interested in learning about this prejudice toward farmers in Haiti. After all, my paternal grandparents were farmers, and I thought they were the best people I had ever met.

My dad would expound further on the misunderstood Haitian population, but at the end of the day, Port-Au-Prince was so over-crowded because people were looking for opportunities, and no one wanted to be called a farmer or planter, even though most of the educated teachers, doctors, lawyers and other professional people in Port-Au-Prince came from families of farmers like my dad. The stigma that invoked the most shame upon them was also the same stigma that made it possible for their parents to finance their education to become doctors, lawyers, teachers, engineers, and so on. If you asked me, it all sounded backwards. Nobody wants to eat GMO products. I ate the best fruits, vegetables, and natural foods while I was in Haiti for those two weeks.

Anyway, after spending those two weeks filled with love with my family in Haiti, I knew the cycle of poverty would be nonexistent through the next generation in our family, as far as my parents were concerned. My grandparents on both sides sacrificed everything to offer the best lives possible to my parents, so I knew my parents didn't want their struggles to become my own struggles, or even their grandchildren's struggles in life. Unfortunately, too many black people have normalized poverty, and have accepted it as a rite of passage for different generations. No matter how extreme a poverty-stricken situation black people face, they're always willing to make the adjustments to adapt to it. That should never be the case. The famous saying, "What doesn't break me makes me stronger," is the biggest crock of shit mentality that black people can subscribe to. You're not supposed to become resilient because white people have turned poverty into a religion for so many of us. The adjustments that black people have made worldwide to justify poverty are unfathomable. After I was able to experience my parents' humble beginnings, I gave thanks to my grandparents for all the sacrifices they made to ensure a better future for my parents. I'm also lucky to have parents who understand and treasure the experiences provided by their own parents, and knew their job as my parents was to help me elevate the family even further.

As an adult, throughout my limited travels around the world, I have witnessed the standards that white people have established for themselves, even while living in African and Caribbean countries. They don't subscribe to poverty. They are always part of the upper echelon, even if it's at the expense of the local people's discomfort, so I have a hard time with the fact that black people have accepted poverty as part of their destiny, which is set by white people and fake black leaders, acting as puppets for white imperialism all over the world. It's not uncommon to hear black people talk about eating mayonnaise sandwiches with sugar water while growing up, and thinking they've made great strides from that, because they can now add Kool-Aid to the sugar water for flavor, and bologna to the mayonnaise sandwich for a better taste. My parents envisioned something entirely different for me. They wanted to leave behind a legacy that will serve as a financial cushion and a springboard for me and my children. The eradication of poverty within my family remained constantly in the forefront of my parents' minds. My dad was especially conscious of the effects of poverty, because of his own upbringing and all the prejudices he faced as a poor farming country boy. My dad made sure that I learned to defend myself against the bullies. He taught me everything he knew and learned as a martial arts student when he was in Haiti. I didn't worry about people putting their hands on me, but the teasing was unbearable at times. I might've gotten into a few fistfights as a result of the teasing when I was younger.

My parents came from a custom where most people paid a seamstress or a tailor and a shoemaker to make their everyday clothing, as well as school uniforms, shoes, and other types of clothing needed for special occasions, such as weddings. The majority of Haitians in Haiti cannot walk into a department store to shop, because they can't afford it. Local seamstresses and tailors earned their living with the support of the local people who commission their talent to create their own designs for any style of clothing. Most Haitian tailors or seamstresses can pretty much emulate any style or design of clothing upon seeing it, so most people usually bring a picture of the sample item they want to have made, the seamstress or tailor usually customizes it to their liking, according to my parents. It's a whole different culture in Haiti. Brand names were something my parents only became aware of when they moved to the United States, and you can trust that they've paid absolutely no mind to it. Brand names were also not a big deal for the general population in Haitian society. Most people in Haiti are too caught up with life's daily struggles and survival to be worrying about some damn brand they can't afford. Their primary goal is to provide a basic meal, shelter, and education for their children, not to be worried about somebody's damn name on something they are wearing. Still, American influence permeates the entire world, so when some Haitians from the Diaspora travel back home for the occasional vacation, they do expose the local people to the name brands that are popular in America. Unfortunately, the people in Haiti are quick to ask for those name-brand items as gifts, without knowing and understanding that their family members are often struggling to afford them in the States.

No other group of people promotes white supremacy and imperialism than black immigrants and African-Americans. It doesn't matter if they're from the Caribbean or Africa, most of them glorify anything white, and they act like America, Canada and any country in Europe is the best place to live. Most African-Americans who live in the white suburbs can't wait for the opportunity to brag about the safety and peace they enjoy in those communities. This constant promotion of white supremacy, of course, has its biases. The black immigrants usually boast about the economies of these first world countries and the amenities they have accessible to them that their own country lack, without realizing the reason why these first world countries in Europe and the West are so developed, is because most of them have a history of exploiting black labor through slavery, they've exploited the resources of the countries they colonized, they've created instability though civil and gang wars by arming and financially supporting warlords and gang members to reinforce insecurity and destabilization, and furthermore, these European allies in cahoots with America and Canada, usually force economic strongholds onto the necks of these countries and the puppet leaders they set in place to reinforce their economic interests abroad.

These black immigrants often believe the white media's narrative that their country is poor or shitty, without the basic understanding that their resource-rich countries are being pillaged by the West, with reinforcement from the street gangs they've armed and financed. In addition, those black immigrants usually travel home with all their expensive clothing, jewelry, and money they often have to borrow, just so they can live lavishly for a couple of weeks to impress their own countrymen and force the impression that America or these European countries have streets that are paved with gold. Sometimes they lie about their education and profession, just for the sake of lying to impress. They seldom tell the truth about the difficulties of assimilating into a new culture, their language barrier, the racism they face, and the struggles to find a job when they first arrive in America or any country in Europe. Most immigrants go home and act like they live in a mansion abroad and they have a cushioned job waiting. They don't tell the truth about their personal experiences, which in fact is a promotion of white supremacy. They usually paint a picture of perfection and bliss, as it relates to America, Canada, France, Great Britain, and the other popular countries they like to emigrate to in Europe. It's usually a total abomination of the truth. At the end of the day, they end up buying into a dream that was forced because of the nightmare created by the West in their homeland.

Dreams are fragmented, while delusions are developed, because capitalism, racism, imperialism and white supremacy are all interchangeable. The black immigrant's own delusion is that his country is no longer worthy of praise ahead of his emigrated country because he found opportunities in abundance. Still, those opportunities are limited because of racism and capitalism. I've heard of educated doctors who left their own practices in their own country, only to move to America to take a job as a dishwasher at a restaurant or janitor, because the US Education Department doesn't recognize those degrees from African and Caribbean countries. Doctors are usually prominent and affluent, no matter where they are from.

Oftentimes, these people have to perpetuate a fraud by buying into a lifestyle they can't afford, in order to maintain their image after moving here. I don't want to single out the doctors, but most immigrants have perpetuated a lifestyle in the states to convince those people back in their home country that they are living a better life abroad. Just like their African-American brethren, some of these people adopt the consumerist mentality. However, that mentality is only enforced when they go back home for a visit. A lot of immigrants are good about saving their money and investing in a home. They still face the same obstacles and adversities that African-Americans face, nonetheless.

Some African-Americans would often completely forgo the white man's history of slavery and their own marginalization after they've managed to earn college degrees. They suddenly start to believe they're pulling themselves by their own bootstraps at the urging of the white man, without realizing they were barefoot before having to work twice as hard to try the level a playing field that will never be leveled, regardless of their higher education. The pay scale based on race and education can justify that. Instead of these educated Negroes staying in their own community to become the examples and beacon of hope for the next generation coming up behind them, they usually pack their belongings and move to the suburbs for safety, without realizing the danger and threat that they grew up around in their own community was created and orchestrated by the same white people who are labeling members of their community threats to society. However, whenever these white folks decide to come back and gentrify the communities that these black people ran from to be closer to the city, their municipalities and police departments suddenly discover the solutions to crime and other ills that plagued the community when black people were the primary residents. These new black suburbanites often find it easier to deal with racism daily at the hands of white people who oppose their presence in those communities, instead of fixing their own communities where they spent their lifetime among people who recognized their names. In addition, they usually face harassment by police while driving or walking in suburban communities, because their skin becomes the identifier that says they don't belong. Still, most people believe capitalism is about choices. Most of us believe we have the free will to live where we want to live and do what we want to do, as long as we can afford the upgrades.

Too many African-Americans have bought into their consumerism practices, and in the process have become insolvent in a country that has marginalized them since the beginning of time. We have seen the surging of so many different brands owned by white companies through braggadocio Hip Hop lyrics that promote brands that seventy-five percent of black people cannot afford. Some people don't understand that "Moving on up" also means acquiring more debt. We live in a debt-driven society, and African-Americans are at the top of the food chains. These companies count on the 1.3 trillion dollars of spending power from the African-American community. It's not by accident that we are targeted. Everything they do is strategic to make sure we stay in a cycle of poverty, while they enrich themselves at our expense. Most young NBA and NFL draft picks are immediately surrounded by white agents, white managers, white accountants, white lawyers, and very little black presence, except for those dependents waiting to help squander the riches of these athletes. The black dollar is recycled right back into the hands of the white people who write the big checks. We don't place too much emphasis on the side of capitalism that takes advantage of our talent and our riches.

We simply view these people as part of our team, and they are supposed to look out for us when we are rich and professional. That is the consumer mindset that is crippling all black people in the community, regardless of their level of income. We feel like we should be able to buy anything that our money can afford. Some athletes and celebrities don't even balance their own checkbooks or manage their own bank accounts. They like to brag about calling their accountants whenever they need to make a big purchase. Only a fool would give someone full access to his money, but that's our tendency as black people to allow others in our entourage to take care of our basic needs. Capitalism is an illusion, and money tends to create delusions for those people who came from nothing.

Getting back to this capitalist society that we live in, which is all about racism, branding, excess, and greed. Unfortunately, the bad habits of these capitalists are spreading worldwide. Capitalist society forces skilled workers into factories like robots to mass produce items branded with a particular name for consummation. However, it's different in Africa, Haiti, and other islands in the Caribbean. The seamstresses and tailors in Haiti who make clothing for people don't have the right to tag their name anywhere on the people's clothing that they are paid to make. To add anything personal on the clothes that they are paid to make, they would need consent from the person paying for the clothes. Mass production of fashion with brand names used to be more of a European and Western culture thing. Most immigrants just care about their children being clothed, fed, getting an education, and maximizing their opportunities wherever they are. The brands don't matter to most immigrant families. While I did receive more of a lesson in Haiti to appreciate the limited privileges that I have as an American-born child to immigrant parents, I also learned that America has set up privileges worldwide for their white citizens, which indirectly benefits all American citizens abroad. Everything America owns is still built on slave labor. The practice is a little different now, because the low wages they pay to employees working in so many American factories throughout third world countries and those that I saw in Haiti, can be justified by the cost of living, something they often establish and also force down the throats of people living in third world countries. From Major League Baseball, to Levi Strauss, I saw thousands of people leaving these factories after a long day's work, walking many miles to get home, because they couldn't afford the fare for a "kamionet" ride from their job to their homes. The low wages paid to these workers could barely keep them afloat financially. I'm also using the word home loosely in this scenario, because most of those people working at these factories can't really afford decent housing. A "kamionet" ride costs barely a couple of Haitian gourds, which is less than fifty cents in US currency, but these workers have to make a choice between a meal or a long walk home every day. In addition, I know the media often show these colorful buses that Haitians refer to as "Tap Tap" on television, but these "Tap Taps" also known as "kamionets," pretty much sustain the livelihood of many families in Haiti. While the public relies on these privately-owned "kamionets" as a mode of transportation, the drivers of these vans/buses usually rely on their 12-hour daily shift of driving these colorful buses up and down the same route, sometimes for as long as it takes to make a profit, in order to provide for their families. Not every driver of those "kamionets" is an owner.

The rigged economic system in Haiti affects mostly the poor. In addition, I also witnessed the disparity in the privileged treatment US passport carrying American citizens received and how Haitian passport carrying citizens are treated at the airport, while returning to their homeland for a visit. Almost all the American citizens zoomed right through customs, while most of the Haitian citizens are held for a longer period of time for questioning and interrogation. Imagined being looked over in your own country, because you carry a passport from your country?

According to my dad, the US, France, and Canada are the biggest culprits behind the dire poverty-stricken conditions I observed throughout Haiti. The US government has basically managed to turn Haiti into a plantation where they get to dictate everything, including the national wage for the country, which is surmountable to the control of the lives of Haitians. The chosen and volunteer Haitian puppets usually line up to exploit their own people and the country's resources for personal gain every five years during the election. One specific former puppet/president that the entire world should know about, is the popular Haitian musician named Michel "Sweet Micky" Martelly. This asshole was the puppet in chief specifically chosen by the Clintons to help squander Haiti's resources. For now, "Tchoul Blan," Michel Martelly, Uncle Ruckus, Sambo, and House Negro are all synonymous. Martelly, his family, and his co-conspirators became very wealthy at the expense of mass poverty, destitution, instability, high crime rates, kidnappings, gang infestations, and the total devastation of Haiti. He also helped to squander the Petro Caribe Fund assistance provided by Venezuela to help sustain the Haitian economy when Haiti needed help, when the US government didn't want to provide any.

The Clintons also benefitted from Martelly's theft to the tune of millions. Bill Clinton has always been a wolf in sheep's clothing, but black folks, even in the United States have been too blind to understand the cons of this racist, murderous, trailer park piece of shit white trash and his even filthier wife. He was the worse piece of shit president that black people could have ever voted for behind Barack Obama. In Haiti, power is purchased, and America is always at the front of the line to bid one of their Negro puppets to exploit the country. Puppet clowns usually line up like slaves at an auction waiting for a bid, so they can become the next "tchoul blan" to exploit Haiti on behalf of the colonizers. It's as if they all are willing to take a pledge to represent the best interest of America, France, and Canada, to help squander the resources of Haiti to these super powers every 5 years. The presidency is usually guaranteed during these fake elections, which are usually financed and monitored by their oppressors in America, France, and Canada. America has always managed to throw a last-minute horse in the race that always comes out of nowhere to emerge victorious during these elections. These racist imperialists have dictated the leadership of Haiti for decades now, but for some odd reason the Haitian people in Haiti and a lot of Haitians in the Diaspora continue to see America as their ally. Hillary Clinton has even fought to force the Haitian government to maintain slave wages in Haiti that benefit American companies in Haiti, as Secretary of State. These filthy corrupted Haitian politicians should be hung publicly to set an example for future US puppets who think they can oppress their own people, in order to serve their US masters.

I may not have been as observant as I should've been while visiting Haiti as a young lady, but my father took every opportunity to help open my eyes to all the injustice that was going on in Haiti, while we were visiting there. My dad always made my education in all areas and on all levels, a priority. My visit to Haiti was a lesson, indeed, because I saw how my parents' cultural norms were so different from the norms they had forced themselves to assimilate into in America. Despite the extreme poverty that I witnessed in some of the places in Haiti, the people there were still kind, proud, and hopeful. At the same time, my father also exposed me to the opulent lifestyles and the extreme wealth that some of the oligarchs enjoyed in Haiti, while closing their eyes to the struggle of the masses that they see every day, on their way to their businesses in town. People greeted us everywhere we went, and almost everyone was cordial and friendly in the provincial part, where my dad came from. Most people knew my dad on a personal level almost, even though he had been gone for a while, and they mostly referred to him by his last name, which is a common practice in Haiti. It's funny that the first free black republic in the world can't see the irony in using people's last name to acknowledge their presence, last names that were forced upon many of my ancestors that my family still carries to this day. A lot of people were happy that my father had made it out of Haiti, for some reason. Some of them wished they could be as blessed as him to get a visa to America. Little did they know what awaited my dad when he first got to America?

Even though we were not rich in America, my father had brought gifts for almost everyone in his neighborhood that he grew up with, and could remember. Even if it was just a pair of socks, the people appreciated everything he gave to them. I no longer wondered why my parents brought so many suitcases when we were leaving for Haiti. They were bringing their goodwill with them in those suitcases. I also wondered why so many of the other Haitians checking in for the flight to Haiti from New York were dragging so many suitcases behind them. My father had to explain to me that most Haitians don't get to go to Haiti often, so when they do go, they try to take care of the entire family, and sometimes friends too, while they're there, so they bring a lot of gift items back with them. However, my father also reiterated and cautioned that some Haitians tend to cultivate this false image of America and other foreign countries that they might've emigrated to, whenever they return to Haiti for vacation. Oftentimes, they sell these people on a false dream about America as the land of opportunity. Before my father moved to America, he thought the same way, because so many Haitians had glorified life in America, without talking too much about the struggles they face as immigrants when they first arrive in any foreign country. My dad was very upfront and honest with anybody who had questions about his life in America. He told them about the difficult transition to a new culture and the less-than-stellar dose of racism he experienced because of the color of his skin, as well as the prejudice he endured at the hands of people who looked just like him but were known as African-Americans. I sat there and listened to him talk about the many factors, such as racism, cultural differences, language barriers, lack of professional skills, or Haitian professional degrees and training that are not accepted by these countries.

My dad never left any stone unturned when he was educating me. It was bit redundant, maybe that was just his way of reinforcing the fact that I should never forget where I came from and my heritage. My father would divulge more details and go more in-depth about the struggles of Haitian immigrants later, after we boarded the airplane. Our short journey from baggage claim to the car was reminiscent of a scene from Coming To America, but the only difference was, we were not royalty in any way. Our bloodline might have been from royalty back in Africa, but we were fighting to become a middle class family in New York.

The celebration started right away when my dad got to his hometown of St. Marc. There were the celebratory hugs and kisses from my grandparents because they hadn't seen him in so long. Of course, I received my own salutation from them, and I could see the excitement on their faces for meeting their granddaughter for the first time. They were also happy to meet my mother, their daughter-in-law, for the first time. It seemed like my dad brought gifts for the entire neighborhood, which included clothing, toothbrushes, toothpaste, shoes, and other basic necessities. My father took his time to hand out marbles to all the children, because playing marbles during the summer is a national pastime in Haiti. My father's town felt like a true community. My dad was paraded to every neighbor's house to greet them, because it's customary in Haitian culture. However, my mother's neighborhood was a little different. City folks are different all around the world. I didn't expect it to be an anomaly in Haiti. Though the people were friendly, they weren't as friendly as the people in the countryside where my father's family lived. Most of the people my mother knewbefore she left Haiti had migrated abroad, and only a handful of them were still around that my mother recognized, when she went back to her old neighborhood for a visit. It was mostly close friends and family who came by to see my mother. My grandmother was trying to keep her visit a secret from many of the people in her neighborhood because she didn't want to experience any jealousy or envy from the neighbors, or worse, an unfortunate kidnapping. After the illegal removal of President Jean Bertrand Aristide by the US government in 2004, kidnappings were rampant in Haiti, and they indiscriminately kidnapped anyone available with a little bit of money. There's a fable in Haiti that "a person should never share their joy with their neighbor, because the neighbor might use Vodou to take away that joy."

We all know that's bullshit, but my mother seemed to have subscribed to it. I never asked why, but that's what she did. She seemed afraid of everything and everyone while we were in Haiti. My dad had to check her a few times, while she acted as if she wasn't born and bred in Port-Au-Prince.

I was happy to meet my grandparents on both sides of my family. My grandparents spoiled the hell out of me the entire time I was there. I couldn't get enough food, hugs, and kisses, and every single one of my favorite meals was cooked by one of my grandmothers every single day, depending on whose house I was visiting. I was treated like a princess during my entire visit. I experienced love on a different level. For people who lived modest lives, with very little luxury, my grandparents were very generous. Well, my maternal grandparents were more upper middle class, according to Haitian standards, as they could afford a lot more material things than my paternal grandparents. Every time I talk about my first visit to Haiti, I get more than a little excited, because that kind of nostalgia is rare, and it makes me proud to embrace my culture.

My first trip to Haiti was also the first time that both of my parents were meeting their in-laws. As a child, I could only observe, but there was a stark difference between my mom's family and my dad's family. My paternal grandparents were definitely a lot more humbled and down to earth. My mother was embraced right away by them and they welcomed her with open arms into the family.

However, I sense a little bit of ambivalence on the part of my maternal grandparents when they first met my dad. It was as if they were expecting someone different, or of a higher class. Right away, I took notice of the housekeeper that my maternal grandparents had at their beck and call, and another young man who managed the yard and ran errands for them. My maternal grandparents barely lifted a finger to do anything. They were always calling on the housekeeper and the errand boy to do everything for them. That was shock and awe to me, because I didn't grow up with that in New York. My maternal grandparents seemed a lot more polished, educated, and business oriented. I was watching and learning, because I knew that I would have plenty of questions later for my parents. I was treated with the same love nonetheless, by both sides of my family. However, there was a sense of gratitude that seemed more genuine that I experienced from my paternal grandparents. I never understood the concept of country folks versus city folks, until I went to Haiti. Country folks are just kinder, gentler, and more loving all around. Anyway, both sides of my family decided to come together at my maternal grandparents' house in the capital city of Port-Au-Prince for a meet-and-greet dinner, before we left Haiti. Let's just say, I would have rather skipped over that part, because it was not necessarily the most positive experience for my mother or my father. Only the strength of their love kept them together after that dinner. All the prejudices of city versus country, educated versus uneducated, and so many other bullshit that keep black people divided all over the world, came to light at that dinner. My grandparents damn near broke up my parents' marriage, because they couldn't accept their differences, but my father was able to pull everyone together to maintain a cordial environment for the dinner. After that debacle, I don't think my grandparents would ever come together again. Good thing my parents lived away from them in the States.

For some odd reason, my maternal grandparents had different expectations of my dad, when they first met him. Let's just say physically he wasn't their cup of tea. My father is a very dark-skinned man with strong features, while my mother is more on the caramel side of the brown paper bag. I don't think his complexion alone was the problem, because I was almost certain that my mom had sent pictures of him with her back home to my grandparents, but apparently not. Surely they saw my pictures, I thought. My complexion is closer to dark than caramel, and I look a lot more like my father than my mom. These grandparents were loving on me too damn much, for them to have some type of prejudice toward my dad, I wondered. Still, words were exchanged, and a lot of it I didn't understand. Without rehashing too many of the stupid prejudices that keep black people apart and divided during that argument, I found ignorance on both sides of my family that I had never seen on display from either of my parents. I was happy to know that my parents had broken a bad cycle that didn't need to linger with me. Apparently, my dad's rural/country upbringing was a problem for my mother's family. As far as I know, my dad has always been a well-mannered gentleman. So, I wasn't sure what my paternal grandparents' objection was. It was definitely a teaching moment for me, and a lesson that my parents taught their own parents that people from different backgrounds can find common ground in their blackness to fall in love. My parents were too strong as a couple to allow a moment of interruption at a family dinner to split them apart. They stood as a unit and tried their best to strip all of my grandparents of their prejudices through conversation. Another lesson learned from my parents.

KANE IS FALLING

Falling in love with Candace was the easy part, because she's so easy to love. I have never met a woman so caring and so willing to please me, and cater to my needs in every way. This was an anomaly for me, and I couldn't even believe women like her exist. Not that I was necessarily searching for a wife at the time, but greatness fell on my lap and I was hooked. I started imagining myself doing all types of activities with Candace, including long walks at the park, overseas vacations, going to sleep with her every night, waking up to her every morning, creating the perfect family with her, holding her in my arms forever, and so much more. I even daydreamed about us sitting next to one another in our rocking chairs on the front porch of our home, while sipping lemonade years down the line. That was not even the extent of how profound my love for Candace had become. I didn't want to live another day without her. Still, I realized that our cultural differences may pose a threat to our relationship, based on prejudices that are rooted in slavery, and created by the oppressors to keep black people divided. My family getting along with hers was a big deal to me. My mother was not the most open-minded person. Although she lived in Boston all her life, had interacted, and even went to school with many black immigrants from the Caribbean and Africa, that didn't help erase some of her prejudices and ignorance. She would say ignorant shit out loud around the house, whenever a random person of immigrant background would piss her off, and a lot of shit she would say was out of character. I never really understood or paid much attention to the depth of her verbal lashes until I met Candace. I had to work on my mother before I brought Candace home to meet her. I didn't want her to assume Candace was African-American, and for her to have one of her prejudiced moments about black immigrants openly in front of her, thinking it was okay. My dad wasn't like that, because there were so many Jamaican, Trinidadian, Cape Verdean, and Puerto Rican females at his high school that he dated prior to meeting my mother. He even dated a Haitian girl in high school before he met my mom. I worried that my mom might embarrass me, once she learned of Candace's Haitian background. She could be very rude at times, and sometimes she didn't know when to hold back or keep quiet when necessary.

While growing up, I had heard some very ignorant statements from my mother in reference to some of our West Indian neighbors who lived across the street, but my dad not so much, because he's more of the big Teddy bear quiet type who likes to get along with everyone. My father is a diplomat and a peacemaker, but my mother is the total opposite. I don't know if my mother acted the way she did because she knew that her husband is big and intimidating-looking to the world, but I supposed her sense of security from my father probably makes that the case. My mother would say unnecessary shit about West Indians whenever she was having a bad day, while having a bad encounter with any of them. She didn't necessarily sort out a particular group, because her venom was toward all immigrants. Then again, in all honesty, I can just say that my mother can be an asshole sometimes. I shouldn't call my mother names, but I've witnessed her behavior all my life, and she's always over the top with everything. Sometimes I wonder how my father has managed to love her for so long. She's my mother, so I have no choice but to love her, but my dad had to learn to love her. She would curse out anybody who crossed her, whether West Indian, white, Hispanic or African-American. I can't even recall the amount of times she chastised the young African-American boys who used to play ball at the park, using the N word to denigrate them for no reason, and verbally insult and even annihilate their spirit sometimes. Most of the people on my block were afraid of my mother. She was the one lady that nobody wanted to mess with. I guess that's probably one of the reasons why I love my mother so much. Her strength and fearless attitude commanded respect.

Still, I understood her strength and fearless attitude didn't erase or overcome her ignorance at times. My mother had to be the tough one, because my dad was so soft-spoken, and she felt as if she was raising kids in a jungle, and she needed to protect her cubs from the predators. One of my best friends, Leon, was from Jamaica, and often times I had to check my mother whenever she was saying some disparaging bullshit about Jamaicans around Leon. I really don't know what it was with my mom that made her like that, because she had been around black people from different parts of the world ever since she was a child in Boston. If I were to guess, I would say Boston is probably one of the highest immigrant populated towns in the northeast behind New York City. The West Indian carnival alone that is held on Seaver Street and Blue Hill Avenue in the Roxbury and Dorchester section of Boston every year is evidence of that. There's a strong West Indian community in Boston, and they have helped the city and the black community thrive over the years. I'm not exactly sure why my mother has never opened her mind to her West Indian neighbors as she should, but I know I was not going to let her ruin my relationship with my Haitian queen, Candace.

Candace was just different than any other woman that I had ever dated. She always made sure that I had a good meal to eat, even when we didn't live together yet. She would come to my apartment and cook for me all the time. Every time we talked on the phone, her first question was always, "Did you eat today, babe?" Her nature was different, and she cared for me in a way I had never experienced before. She was very nurturing and loving. There were many other things that Candace did that I can't even describe. If I ran out of shower gel, she would show up at my apartment with shower gel, deodorant, toothpaste, or whatever it was that was missing. She would do my laundry without me asking and did things that made me believe she was properly groomed to be a wife by her mother. I'm not insinuating that women must be domesticated to be good wives, but Candace had my heart because she was so domesticated and caring at the same time. I don't think she was giving me wifey vibes to get a ring, it was just her nature. Nonetheless, she gave me a glimpse of what was to come, if we ever got married. And I loved how my future with her looked. Everything she did for me was appreciated. I just couldn't let a woman like that get away from me. She actually reminded me a little bit of my mother, but a sweeter and toned down version. Though my mother had a smart mouth and she would sometimes say things to my father to test her limits with him, but she was also nurturing, caring, and very loving toward him. My dad was the one person that my mother never flipped on. She had a level of respect for him that I never saw her display toward anybody else. I could never understand how she was able to keep her attitude in check when it came to my father. My father was her light and rock, and she acknowledged it all the time. My mother would fight for that man and her family. She didn't play when it came to her marriage. Most people on the outside don't know that side of my mother. Her feminine and nurturing side remains a secret to outsiders. My father is a very patient man. He managed to develop his own coping mechanism and style to deal with my mother over the years. Nothing she has done to him has gotten under his skin, and he always has her back. He is very patient with her, and he would always remind us as children, "You know your mother," meaning she was stubborn and nothing to play with, but she loved us with every fiber of her being. I knew that my mother loved me very much and cared about my happiness more than anything. As long as she was aware of the level of love I had for Candace, she would be able to manage to keep her ignorance in check... I'd hoped, anyway.

Bringing Candace to Boston to meet my parents was something that I struggled with, simply because of my mother. My mother and I never had a discussion about her rudeness toward immigrant folks, but I'm guessing she might've had a negative personal encounter with somebody at some point in her life, and has allowed it to taint her mind to the point where she thought they were taking over Boston, and Black people were going to be pushed out of their own community. The irony in all of this is the fact that Black people had been here years before the immigrants arrived, and if African-Americans really wanted the menial jobs that most immigrants are willing to do when they first get here, those positions would've been taken over by African-Americans a long time ago. The anti-immigrant sentiments are rooted in racism, even though white people were the first immigrants to invade all the continents around the world. Some black folks, unfortunately, have adopted the wicked ways of their master, without understanding that white people's abhorrent treatment of other people is rooted in control and racism. Some people like to say a lot of shit just to stir the pot to make themselves feel better, most of the time. I learned from Candace that most immigrants from the Caribbean would accept almost any job when they first get here, in order to find a way to provide for their family here and back home. That's an honorable trait. I'm sure nobody wants to cross the ocean to come here to clean toilets. I'm not saying that all West Indians do that, but having heard the stories from Leon and Candace, most West Indians are proud people with vision, and they would do whatever it takes to take care of their family. I needed to make sure that my mother understood that. Then again, I had been gone for a while, anything could've transpired in my absence. Perhaps my mom had matured a little in my absence, right?

Completely opposite from the relationship that I have with my mom, is the relationship that I share with my dad. I have a different type of bond with him. He is my dude, meaning I can go to him with anything, and he'd always give me feedback objectively, without injecting his personal views to influence anything I want to do. I really love that about my dad. Most people believe that sons are supposed to be closer to their mothers than their fathers, but that's not the case with me and my dad. I was always a daddy's boy. I wanted to be around my father all the time, and he took me everywhere with him. My dad was the fun parent. My mom was more of a disciplinarian and tyrant. My mom wanted to make sure none of her children ended up a statistic. She was hard on us. My dad wanted to make sure that I was reared properly as an Alpha male. He always told me that alpha males aren't bothered by the trials and tribulations women put them through. As long as I stand my ground and show leadership when it's necessary, my action will dictate the behavior of any woman. He always respected my decisions, but guided me whenever he felt I needed guidance. My dad is primarily responsible for the man that I have become today, and I'm grateful for that. He may seem a little passive with my mom, but he's every bit of an Alpha male that you can find. He's only soft when it comes to her, but she doesn't get to walk all over him. He has put her in her place many times, and she knows when she can't push back and cross the line with him. I've also seen my dad's disposition publicly on many occasions, while defending and protecting my mom. No one would dare disrespect my mom in the presence of my dad. He is a sure Alpha. I love the big guy.

My parents made sure that my siblings and I had a great childhood. They didn't do too much sugarcoating to shield us from the reality of the world. My mom was always the nurturer and most of the times the disciplinarian as well, which created conflict for us at times. One minute she wanted to whoop our asses, and the next minute she was hugging us. My dad always had the final words, and made the final decision when it came to our family. That's the one line my mother never crossed. She allowed my dad to be the king of his castle, and he always treated her like a queen. My father always said, "You can't expect to be treated like a king if you're not willing to acknowledge your queen." I just needed my queen mother to let go of her prejudices, and embrace my new love. I was hoping that she could surprise me in the most positive way with her actions when she finally got a chance to meet Candace.

CANDACE'S
FAMILY JOURNEY

My struggles were a little different from Kane's. I'm a product of two immigrant parents who moved to the United States from Haiti to escape many different struggles, including persecution, civil rights violations, famine, high unemployment, and so many other factors, due to US manipulation of the Haitian economy and Haitian society as a whole. When the ship my dad boarded in Haiti landed on the shores of the port of Miami, he was elated to have made it safely from Haiti, and escaped the grip of malfeasance, dictatorship, instability, intimidation, and forced poverty from his small town of Saint Marc. As a kid, Jean Francois Joseph, my dad, dreamed of becoming a civil engineer, and he wanted to be the first developer to make the development of his hometown a priority, and to turn Saint Marc into a tourist hub like no other town in Haiti. He used to daydream about erecting unique architectural buildings all over Saint Marc, and building residential communities with lots of schools and an electrical grid that would provide electricity around the clock to the town, so the kids from his hometown didn't have to move, or travel back and forth daily to Port-Au-Prince to attend the better schools in order to get a good education, like he had to do. My dad spent his earlier years attending school at Maitre Hillaire's elementary school, and then he moved on to Frere Herve De Saint Marc to complete 6th through 8th grade. After completing the 8th grade, my dad realized the better secondary schools were in Port-Au-Prince, and he needed to move there to study, because the daily commute to Saint Marc would be too long.

My dad's family wasn't rich by the definition of wealth, but my grandparents were rich culturally, and knew how to save a penny or two to achieve a goal. They managed to save up enough money to send my dad to Port-Au-Prince, the capital of Haiti, to attend the esteemed Lycee Petion at the time. Though Lycee Petion was a public school, it offered one the best education in Haiti, public or private. Back when my dad was a child, Haiti's public "Lycees" or secondary schools, were the best. Public schools in Haiti are very different from public schools in the States where children are given free meals, free textbooks, and they don't have to wear uniforms or pay any fees to attend school. In Haiti, the parents have to pay for the uniforms, the meals, the textbooks, and the monthly cost of school tuition, though the tuition is usually lower than private schools. Of course, being from a small town, the move to Port–Au-prince was a little challenging for my dad at first, but he managed to adjust, according to him. Moving from a small town to a big city can be a difficult transition for anybody. My dad was no different. In his small town of Saint Marc, almost everybody knew his name, who he was, and who his parents were. They had seen him grow up right before their eyes, just like many of the other children in his community. All the mischievous children were known to everybody and the cerebral ones as well. My dad belonged to the latter group. My grandparents didn't think it was a gamble when they decided to pay for my dad's lodging, where he stayed at a family friend's house in Port-Au-Prince, sharing a small room with the family's son, while sleeping in a single bed. They sent huge barrels of food for him monthly that lasted until the next delivery arrived. You name it, they sent it. From big bags of rice, sizable containers of dry beans, oil, cornmeal, fresh fruits, and more, so he could be treated fairly by the hosting family, and not want for anything during his stay for the school year. The hosting family was more than happy to welcome everything that my grandparents could afford to send for my father every single month, without ever missing a beat. Country folks have a sense of pride that may not be prevalent in city folks. My grandparents wanted my father to walk with his head high, and to remember his roots. My grandparents were very proud people, in spite of what people thought about them. They didn't want to give anybody the opportunity to ostracize or stigmatize their son with denigrating labels, because his parents were farmers and where he came from.

You see, according to my dad, a lot of people in Haiti look down on farmers, because Haitian society has never valued its farmers, and a lot of people in Haiti, due to their lack of education about agriculture, see "farming" as a "frown upon and less desirable" profession. It's not uncommon for Haitians to insult each other by calling a person a "planter, or neg mone," which means mountain Negro, a derogatory name. This name calling is often associated with farming, for public humiliation. Unfortunately, too many Haitians are ignorant of the fact that farmers contribute more to the country's economic growth than any other professionals. They often denigrate and verbally abuse the people involved in the most important and crucial sector of their economy daily. Being called a farmer or planter is one of the most denigrating loud public insults in Haiti. It's all because of the government's lack of involvement in providing mass education on farming and the agriculture industry, as well as prioritizing local foods and products. The government doesn't offer any subsidies to farmers so that local agriculture could be a priority. Farmers are not important to Haitian society, because few of them have received formal education. Farmers themselves don't even understand that they are the backbone of the economy. My grandparents had endured these insults most of their lives whenever they came to the city, so they did everything in their power to create a respectful bubble for my father. People might notice a slight accent that is different from those people who live in the city, and that alone could allow prejudice to prevail. My dad was going to be educated at all costs, as far as my grandparents were concerned. Farming was the last thing they wanted my father to get involved with. They expected him to be better than them, without realizing their own greatness and worth in a society that doesn't even understand their great contribution to their local economy. Most of the doctors, lawyers, engineers, and teachers in Haiti had their education financed with farming money, but too often after they become educated, they turn their backs on the very source of income that provided them with their formal education.

My paternal grandparents, though illiterate only in the traditional formal scholarly way, were very proud and humble people who understood the importance of an education. They never had the opportunity to attend school themselves as children, so they put great effort into making sure that my dad would go further educationally in his life. A formal education was a must. My dad's intelligence was their glory, but his education would solidify their existential happiness on earth. They did everything in their power to ensure my dad was well taken care of by the family friend, and was respected at the same time. My grandparents were born into farming and they were fairly known local farmers who owned a plantain and banana farm with other fruits and vegetables on a 5-acre farm that had been passed down for four generations, since slavery ended in Haiti in 1804 when the Haitians fought for their independence from the colonizing French. A lot of people from the community bought their goods from my grandparents, including vendors who purchase in wholesale quantities for resale.

During my father's infantile years, he consumed a lot of naturally grown foods such as rice and beans, corn, mangoes, cherries, grapes, and other vegetables that were harvested on the farm, and in abundance within the Saint Marc region of the country. My father was a strong young man with a promising future, and my grandparents recognized his potential very early on. My father was also essentially my grandparents' eyes at an early age, due to their illiteracy. He read and explained everything to them whenever it was necessary. At one point in time, it was normal for black families to be limited because of their illiteracy, and were exploited and taken advantage of by the colonizers as a result. It also wasn't unusual for illiterate black people to conceive and rear bright and intelligent children who would grow up to become doctors, lawyers, engineers, scientists, and so on. A lot of people don't understand that illiteracy, for the most part, usually takes place due to lack of opportunity. My grandparents' illiteracy was never a barrier to a better future for their own children.

During colonial slavery, most black people were prevented from learning how to read and write. The colonists made it illegal in many countries for black people to become literate. It was their way of protecting and maintaining their fake superiority. However, the ingenuity of black people can't be denied, no matter where they are in the world. A struggling black single mother can produce a billionaire out of the Marcy projects in Brooklyn in Jay Z. While education was a priority for the children of most illiterate farming parents in Haiti, many of these parents failed to realize that teaching their offspring a trade that they mastered could take them farther than anything their children could've learned in a classroom setting. A formal education alone isn't enough for a child to achieve great things. To this day, a lot of farmers in Haiti are failing to teach their children how to farm, because of the stigma associated with being a farmer. The goal for most farmers is always for their children to achieve more than they were given the opportunity to achieve educationally and professionally, while distancing them from farming. Even in America, many black people who left the plantation completely illiterate after slavery ended, were able to instill certain values, morals, and principles into their children that produced many professionals, including doctors, lawyers, teachers, and other upstanding citizens to serve the newly formed free black communities. Haiti was no different.

My dad would grow up to be the first literate and college educated person in his entire immediate family. My paternal grandparents were forced into farming early in their lives, because they had to help sustain the family financially, as their focus was on the family farm, which was their daily survival possession, and the livelihood of their children, according to the stories that my dad has told me about his family. The land my grandparents owned had cultivated life for four generations of illiterate farmers since Haiti became the first free black republic. It was after the Haitian Revolution that their forefathers secured that land. As brutal as slavery was for all black people who were captured from Africa and brought to the New World, Jean-Jacques Dessalines and Toussaint L'Ouverture would match the brutality of the French, the British, and the Spanish, in order to secure their liberty on the Caribbean island called Hispaniola. My forefathers and all black people benefitted from the Haitian Revolution. According to my grandfather, my immediate ancestors fought in that war as well. Their compensation after the war was the land that they acquired that has been in the family since they became free. After the Haitian Revolution, for many families, it was about survival, reconstruction, and establishing a new country where black people would no longer succumb to the oppressive measures of the European colonizers, in addition to helping to govern a newly liberated country right after slavery ended. There was no transition period. Survival left very little time for anyone to pursue a formal education at the time, but these folks were educated in so many other ways. It was rare that my great-grandparents didn't know a natural cure for any illnesses that anybody in their community may have brought to them. In a way, they served as the unofficial doctors of their community. They also passed that knowledge on to my grandparents, which is useful to this day. My grandparents can call which leaves or fruit to use to cure almost any disease known to mankind. They know everything about natural medicine, something they also passed on to my dad.

WHITE IMPERIALISM
IN HAITI

As a commune of Latibonit or "Artibonite," as it is pronounced in French, in the western part of Haiti, Saint Marc also serves as the port of entry for goods that are imported into Haiti. Opportunities in Saint Marc were abundant, but restricted at the same time. My grandparents could've easily become millionaires, if Haiti had a functional and stable government, less the theft and corruption reinforced by US puppets in Haiti who had been placed in their positions to secure the interests of America. Few people know that Papa Doc actually attended the University of Michigan School of Health, where he was trained to help the US soldiers. It was during his stay in America where he experienced racism of the worse kind that he adopted his Noirist philosophy, and also caught the eyes of the US GOVERNMENT OFFICIAL exploiters. The biggest threat to the US at the time was communist Cuba, and they needed an ally close enough to monitor Cuba. At first, the US government was against the fraudulent election of Duvalier in Haiti, but because the country had stabilized somewhat under his leadership, the US decided to fully back him as a dictator for life. However, there were conditions set forth, in order for him to continue as the lifetime president of Haiti, but Papa Doc also had his own personal agenda, and the US vowed to turn a blind eye to his antics, as long as he protected US interests. After the US government allowed Papa Doc Duvalier to install himself as the dictator-in-chief in the former Pearl of the Antilles, Haiti saw a mass exodus and exile of the country's most intellectual people to other countries in the world, but mostly to the former Francophone colonies in Africa, where most of them became educators at the university and college level. A lot of the Haitian elite and educated individuals were chased out by the Duvalier regime, because Papa Doc didn't value experience and education other than his own at the time. Most of these people fled to the US, Cuba, Canada, France and other countries that benefited more from their prosperous education and experience, while Haiti was left without future leaders, thinkers, professors, and other professionals. Papa Doc was a tyrant who lacked common sense and depth. The US government capitalized on his tunnel vision, and as a result, the exploitation of Haiti began, and the road to turning Haiti into a plantation was mapped out. Papa Doc saw the educated, experienced, and knowledgeable people of Haiti as a threat to his tyranny, because he wanted to lead the blind and uneducated to their destructive faith, without understanding education was key to the development of any country. A

Robinhood pretender, who helped cure many Haitians of yaws, Papa Doc used his popularity to rule with an iron fist.

The mass exodus of highly educated Haitian professionals and intellectuals to other countries set Haiti back almost a century educationally and economically. The reason why so many of these Haitian professionals fled to Francophone countries in Africa, was because the cultural transition was easier without the language barrier to complicate matters. Haitians share the closest culture and customs to African people in the Caribbean, followed by the Jamaicans. Haitians, and Jamaicans for the most part, are very proud of their African ancestry. Many of the affluent Haitians also sought asylum in France to escape the brutality of Papa Doc's wrath against them. The elites always held the key to Haiti's economy, and Papa Doc wanted to put a stop to it, but with a failed and poor plan that sent Haiti into the abyss and a chaotic state economically. The people of the Republic of Congo and the Ivory Coast benefited greatly from the Haitian exiles, as they were able to assimilate very quickly in these countries and helped assist with the educational system there. It was a loss to Haiti but a gain to many other African nations. Many of the civilians who disagreed with the new regime, and Papa Doc's newly established secret police, the Tonton Macoutes, also fled to escape persecution at the hands of those newly installed puppets of the dictator who sought revenge for whatever reason, and who were also violating the rights of every possible human being who didn't support his administration. Papa Doc's dictatorship might've been the worst thing that ever happened to Haiti, because the violations of human rights and life that were supported by the US government. No leader in the Caribbean can proclaim his dictatorship for life without the approval of the US government. Anything that is supported by the racist government in America is guaranteed to work to the detriment of black people. However, more importantly, the United States turned a blind eye to this indignant man and allowed him to run amok, as long as he protected US interest and abused his own people. Haiti could've used the assistance of our brothers and sisters in America to stop US complicity in Haiti, and the slaughtering of many victims who didn't deserve to die. The annihilation of black people has never mattered to the world. We have to be conscious of that fact. Many victimized people in Haiti remained silent to avoid facing execution in the dead of night. Everyone was suspicious, and everyone was a spy, as far as the people were concerned. The US government was nowhere to be found as defenders of human rights in Haiti. This was almost the precursor to the genocide that took place in Rwanda.

While reading books about the genocide in Rwanda, I noticed the similarities. What happened in Haiti was close to genocide, because hundreds of thousands of people lost their lives, and it was practiced and perfected under the leadership of Papa Doc. People were forced to turn against one another for safety reasons, as well as personal access to government perks and protection. It wasn't unusual for Haiti's secret police to invade people's homes in the middle of the night, drag them out of bed, only for them to never be heard from again. Papa Doc's personal Firing Squad saw to it that nobody disagreed with his idiotic ideologies. Unfortunately, after Papa Doc died, his idiot son Jean Claude Duvalier took over the presidency, and continued his reign of terror on the people.

My grandparents were nothing but peasants in the eyes of the government, so they chose to keep quiet. However, my dad wasn't as docile, passive, and submissive as them. My grandparents were not political people, but they knew and understood their place in that society. Still, they were raising a radical son who was educated and understood the injustice that was going on in the country wasn't right or fair. While my grandparents wanted to survive long enough to raise their only son the best way possible, my dad was defiant of the government, and it was a matter of time before they would've come to the house to drag him off in the middle of the night to make an example out of him, to cowardly force him to face a firing squad in some unknown location. My grandparents feared for him daily. He was having discussions with people openly that he shouldn't have had. My grandparents were almost certain his death sentence would show up on their doorstep at any moment. These stories used to make me sad, whenever my dad would divulge them to me. My father sometimes sounded like he was a broken man spiritually, because he'd never done anything to change the direction of the country. Oftentimes, it was when the two of us were alone that my father would tell me about his life in Haiti. These stories used to anger me.

Soon after my dad graduated from Lycee Petion, he was able to gain admission to the state university to study civil engineering. My grandparents couldn't be more happy and proud. An illiterate couple with a son who was about to attend college? It was the reality that my grandparents had been waiting for since my dad was born. Unfortunately, there would be too many obstacles that would prevent my father from achieving his dream. Papa Doc died on April 21st, 1971, right after my dad completed high school. As a former dictator and president for life, his idiot, immature son, Jean Claude "Baby Doc' Duvalier, succeeded him and rose to power at the immature age of 18 years old. The Haitian people didn't push back, because Papa Doc's secret police, the "Tonton Macoutes," were there to ensure a smooth transition of power, while the US government continued to turn a blind eye to the injustice and human rights violations in Haiti. The United States government supported this dictatorship, for as long as the Haitian government made US interests their top priority.

Turning Haiti into a plantation because our ancestors fought valiantly to defeat the French, Spanish, and the British to put a stop to imperialism on the island, was always the goal of all the imperialist nations around the world, which includes France, Britain, Spain, Canada, and The United States. It also took more than a handful of sellout puppets to become pawns in their game, in order to accomplish that feat. There didn't seem to be any light at the end of the tunnel, according to my dad. Haitians didn't get a chance to rejoice when the tyrant dictator, Papa Doc Duvalier, died. Instead, they saw the emergence of another nincompoop young dictator who barely understood his role and position as a leader of the first black republic in the world. Human rights abuses were just as rampant under Baby Doc Duvalier, and the violations were far more excessive, because he had to prove that he could lead at such a young age, though everyone knew the real person who held that power at the time was a general named Jacques Gracia. Baby Doc Duvalier was just a placeholder and a puppet. I could never understand how Jean Claude Duvalier earned the nickname "Baby Doc." He was never a doctor, and only the racists in the Western world could've assigned that moniker to him, to reinforce his fake leadership.

My dad matured under the Baby Doc Duvalier regime, so he barely understood what true freedom was. Though he was always outspoken as a young man, my grandparents did everything in their power to contain his outspokenness, in order to keep him alive. In turn, to keep my grandparents from worrying, my dad spoke his mind in places away from the safety of his home, Due to his love and respect for my grandparents, he also didn't want to bring the danger of being exposed or identified by potential enemies as an enemy of the state. He felt that the Tonton Macoutes could pull up on him at any time, and it would kill my grandparents to never learn of his disappearance.

My dad was very progressive in his thoughts, and he had a vision to change Haiti. Well, at least his hometown of Saint Marc. Unfortunately, his dream to change Haiti would never come to fruition. After graduating with a degree in civil engineering from the state university, my dad, nor my grandparents, had the connection to help him land a job anywhere in Haiti. Whether a person is an educated professional, or an illiterate Tonton Macoute with a gun, Haiti was all about who you know, in order to get anywhere in life. Even though my grandparents' farming business had helped pay his way through school, my father could not see himself farming as an alternative. Not that he held any prejudices against farming or farmers, but he just could not see himself cultivating his parents' land for the rest of his life. He had much bigger dreams. He felt that wasn't his purpose in the world. He was an educated man, living a delusional life in a state-run illusion created by the white imperialists in America, Canada, France, and the rest of the supremacists who run the world. Baby Doc Duvalier was just the next installed puppet of the United States. He was the Negro put in charge, to make sure Haiti continued to pay the price for defeating Napoleon,

Spain, the British army, and debunking the myth of white suprem-acy. My father was always "woke,'" so he was more than aware of what was going on. He recognized quickly there was no future in Haiti for him after he graduated from college at the top of his class. He knew if he stayed in Haiti, he would have a short lifespan, be-cause he couldn't contain the fire in him to fight injustice.

I'd get emotional and tears would well up in my eyes every time I told my dad's story to my husband, and other people who don't understand the struggles immigrants often faced in their home country, and the more difficulties they have to face when they arrive to this country. My dad's dream was deferred, and I wanted to make sure that he saw his reality in me. My grandparents were heart-broken when my dad walked into their small "Ajoupa," (a wood-en-framed house with a thatched roof with enclosed sides) styled home one day, to tell them he was going to leave for America. He had tried to obtain a visa the legal way, but he didn't have the con-nection to get one legally. My father was never the networking type, because he felt most of the people he went to school with were prej-udiced, pompous assholes, who looked down on him, even though he was smarter than all of them. He wanted to do everything his way. After his fourth failed attempt to secure a legal visa to visit the United States, my dad had made up his mind he was gonna get there any way that he could. "After all, the Indians didn't require the British criminals to obtain visas when they invaded America," he used to tell me. In addition, the American government forced an occupation of Haiti in 1915 to ensure its total economic demise, which is why my dad couldn't prosper in his own country to begin with. The first act of theft committed by the US government when their troops invaded Haiti was the looting of the country's gold reserve and national bank. The US government transferred all of the Haitian government's money and gold to Citi Bank in New York City, a bank that paid rebels to destabilize the country. The Haitian constitution at the time forbade foreign nationals to own and purchase land in Haiti, but the invaders changed Haiti's constitution and illegally ratified it to suit them. The US government illegally rewrote the constitution of a sovereign country, and the international community never said a word about it. That's what white imperialism does. Although the US ended up occupying Haiti for 19 years, the Cacos led by Charlemagne Peralte, did not take it lying down. They fought valiantly and killed many American troops. In the end, the US did what they always do around the world to show their racism and fake supremacy after an invasion. After the capture of Charlemagne Peralte, they inhumanely paraded his head on a stick to scare the rest of his followers into laying down their weapons. To this day, Charlemagne Peralte remains one of the modern heroes of Haiti. However, soon after the colonizers changed the constitution, American corporations and the US government began purchasing property and land across Haiti and illegally confiscated as much land as they possibly could with military force, whenever necessary, something that was forbidden by the founding founders of the country, which was clearly written in the original constitution. In my dad's mind, going to America by any means necessary was a form of reparation, because of America's illegal invasion of Haiti, which is still affecting generations of Haitians to this day. Of course, US manipulation of Haiti's economic infrastructure has never stopped, even today. Their goal is to bring Haiti to her knees, but Haitians are resilient and high-spirited people. They're not as fragile as white supremacy.

While my grandparents were saddened by my dad's decision to leave Haiti, they called on their African spiritual guide, Ogun (Papa Ogou), in prayer, to help secure a safe voyage to the States for my dad. My grandparents are true believers in their African spirituality, which is known to most people as Vodou. My dad raised me with the full understanding that Vodou is an African spirituality that has been practiced by his family since the colonizers brought our ancestors to Haiti and tried to indoctrinate them with Christianity. I have never been ashamed of this practice, and I told Kane right up front that I wasn't going to subscribe to any type of white Jesus worshipping if that was his thing. I'm too well aware of my roots to allow anyone to shame my culture and heritage. A lot of people who have been brainwashed by colonization tend to believe Vodou is evil, without paying close attention to the actual evil of Christianity, and those white people who have forced Africans to abandon their own spiritual practices, in order to beat the belief in Jesus Christ into them and handed them a bible, while they stole every natural resource that belonged to Africans. Even in Haiti, a lot of people practice Vodou in secret, because too many of these ignorant fools have allowed their white kidnappers to convince them that their own religion and heritage is bad for them, They have allowed the Catholic and Christian churches to influence their way of life and belief system, which has weakened the culture. The infusion of Catholicism into Vodou was something that the slaves had to do, in order to fool their white master into believing they were practicing the Catholic religion forced upon them, while actually still practicing Vodou. The symbolism and the adoration and admiration of saint-like figures and other images from the Catholic Church were smokescreens to cover up the practice of Vodou in plain sight in front of their captors. It was also the same thing with language. Most of the slaves in the Caribbean developed different variations of patois that derived from the languages of their captors, in order to communicate and to keep the enslavers from understanding what they were saying. However, in the case of Haiti, the revolutionaries idn't want the colonizers to know what they were plotting. Spirituality was always a first priority to the captive Africans, while language was second. My family has always embraced their African heritage, culture, and customs, and my grandparents made sure they passed down the practice to their children. We see the beauty in our culture, but we also see the evil in the deeds of those people who make it their business to subjugate and oppress black people worldwide. Satan's job is to vilify the good people, in order to appear godly.

After my father left for Miami, my grandmother was confident that my father would arrive safely, because the spirit had come to warn her about his voyage way before my dad even decided he was going to leave Haiti for Miami. I guess clairvoyance is a part of spirituality, too. My grandparents knew that they couldn't convince my dad to stay in Haiti any longer, and they also knew leaving Haiti was probably better for him. No, my dad wasn't going to risk his life on a small raft to Miami. My dad's a brilliant man. He was able to make contact with a man who worked for a big export shipping company that shipped goods between Haiti and Miami. The man arranged for my dad to get on the ship for a fee, which was pretty much most of my dad's life savings. It was a risk my father was willing to take, so he could get to the land of milk and honey, as proclaimed by America and those immigrants who often brag about America on television. In addition, the white American tourists who came to Haiti always made America sound like it was paradise. However, Haitian kids use to take the opportunity to tease these white people by referring to them as "blanmanan." I didn't exactly know what that meant when my mother tried to explain it to me. I guess it was kids having fun, as they pointed to the strange-looking white people who were visiting their country, and often walking around half-naked, which was frowned upon in Haitian society back then.

The false narrative that the US is the best country in the world to live is sold to everyone around the world, and my dad was no different. My dad truly believed that he would have a different life, once he arrived in the United States. It didn't help that so many Haitian immigrants would go back home to visit their family, and once there, they would walk around with an aura of superiority, as if the United States had given them a new status and confidence that was above their own people in Haiti. My father would eventually learn after moving to the United States, that most of these Haitians who visited Haiti after immigrating to the United States would adopt the superior attitude that they saw white people using to denigrate black people in America, against their own people back home. In reality, few of these Haitian immigrants were truly living the American dream. He'd learned that many of them were struggling immigrants who had difficulties transitioning to a new culture, and the language barrier made the assimilation to American culture even harder for most of them. In addition, he also learned that it took some of these Haitian immigrants years, and sometimes decades, to change their immigration status to legal, in order to be able to make the trip back to Haiti. By the time they're able to go back home to visit, they would use most of their savings, bring their best outfits back home with them, the best jewelry they have or could borrow from their friends, and everything they've worked hard for over a decade or longer, so they could splurge for two weeks and reinforce this false American dream to other Haitian people, thus creating this mass exodus of Haitians to America. It's not just white people lying about the American dream. Most Haitians who visit Haiti are also reinforcing it by not being honest about their struggles in America. Most of the time, some of these Haitians lie about their professions when they go back home, telling family members they're nurses, doctors, and other professionals, while they are nothing more than a nurse's aide, housekeepers, or working other menial positions that that they are too ashamed to allow family members to know, in order to make ends meet and survive in America. They don't glorify the fact that they sometimes have to rent a room in somebody's basement in New York City to get their start, or that they have to work two full-time jobs, earning minimum wage just to survive. They're often too ashamed to tell their family the truth, because they're often responsible financially for their entire family and many generations of people that rely on them to pull them out of poverty. This situation is not exclusive to Haitians, though. A lot of black immigrants usually flaunt a false lifestyle when they go back home for vacations. The American dream has also become the greatest Haitian nightmare, because most Haitians would sell everything they own to get a visa to come to America, without knowing and understanding they have more value in their own country than abroad. Anyway, my grandparents were able to scrape up some money to help my father finance his voyage to the

United States, because they believed in his dream. They gave him an additional $500.00 US dollars, which was the last savings that they had, for pocket money after he arrived in the States. Back in 1976, $500.00 was enough to rent a room for a couple of months in most places in the States, including New York City.

There was no fanfare when my dad arrived at the Port of Miami on that big ship. He was immediately detained, as he had no legal papers or reason for being in Miami, and was taken to a Guantanamo Bay holding facility near Cuba. He remained there for months, until an advocacy group for human rights in Miami fought on his behalf to be released, so he could legally gain resident status in the United States. It was a long battle, but he eventually obtained his legal papers to work after he was released from the Guantanamo holding facility. For months, my grandparents worried and cried every night, because they hadn't heard from my dad while he was in custody. He had no way of getting words to them that he was all right after he was detained. They had no confirmation that he was dead or alive, but they found comfort in their African spirituality. My grandfather was certain that nothing bad could happen to my dad, because he had his own premonition that my father was okay. The spirits had spoken to him and reassured him that my dad was fine. That's the story I've heard from my dad, and it was confirmed when I went to Haiti for my first visit. While my family was reminiscing about my dad's departure from Haiti, they spilled everything. My grandparents did get word that my dad had made it to Miami safely via the friend who let him on that ship when he first arrived. That was the limited news they had on him. It was a personal favor that my father had asked of the friend because he knew my grandparents would be worried to death.

When my dad finally got out of the detention center, the first thing he did was send a telegram to my grandparents, to let them know that he had been detained for a while, but was out, and was given legal temporary status to live in the United States. My grandparents were overjoyed to confirm that he was fine. My grandmother worried more than my grandfather did. Again, they prayed to the ancestors and asked that they protect my father and bless him in abundance. To cope with the situation, my grandfather adopted the mindset that my dad was going to become a big shot in America, and he was well on his way. The agony of my grandmother's daily worries was enough to drive my grandfather mad, but he was stoic in his position, and told my grandmother not to worry herself to death about a decision their adult son had made. "He's in America now, stop worrying. The spirits, Erzulie Dantor, Erzulie Freda, and Papa Ogou are watching over him. Stop worrying yourself to death. Our prayers work. The ancestors have never failed us," my grandfather would tell her every night before they went to bed to comfort her. "Killing yourself with stress is not going to keep our son alive. Just keep praying to the spirits to protect him, and he shall be ok," he would also say to her. My grandmother made it her daily regimen to talk to her ancestral spirits and guides. She would call on Legba, Dumbala, Papa Gede, Baron Samedi, Carre-fou, Simba, Ogou, Ezili Dantor, Ezili Freda, and all the other spirits that were passed down to her from her ancestors. She would honor, feed, and celebrate the spirits as much as possible and as often as possible, so that they could protect her son. My grandmother was a strong believer in the Vodou spirituality. Her ancestral spirits had never let her down, whenever she called on them for prosperity, protection, safe health, and overall livelihood. Though my grandfather didn't necessarily explore all the spirits on his side of the family as my grandmother did, he did honor them whenever she held her own ceremony. My granddad wasn't necessarily raised in a household that practiced Vodou as a religion openly, but he had been exposed to it behind closed doors. Unfortunately, back in the day, a lot of Haitian families were shamed whenever people learned of their Vodou practice in the community. My granddad became a proud practitioner of his African spirituality ever since he met my grandma. My dad also became an open practitioner of Vodou after he met my mom.

When the folks from France colonized Haiti, they brought with them the myth of werewolves, which translates into "Loup-Garou" in French or "lougarou" in the official Haitian language, which is Kreyol. The mythological "lourgarou" in Haiti is a stigma attached to all Vodou practitioners. Unbeknownst to most Haitians, the French were very afraid of African spirituality during the Haitian revolution. The great Haitian maroon leader, Francois Mackandal, known as a Vodou priest or hougan, joined the Haitian Revolution and became a mythological figure in Haitian history for his knowledge of poison, as well as his valor. He was a fearless leader who was against the enslavement of Africans on the island of Hispaniola, which Haiti shares with the Dominican Republic. Fluent in Arabic, due to his origin (not 100% confirmed) either in Senegal, Mali or Guinea and having practiced the Muslim faith, prior to being sent to Haiti, Mackandal was a hougan who had great knowledge of poisons, and he orchestrated and organized great plots to kill the slave masters and their animal crops by poisoning their water supplies. Slave owners became terrified of him, as he and his followers killed hundreds of slave owners. His poisonous secret was tortured out of a captured slave. Mackandal was the reason the term "black magic" was coined during the Haitian Revolution. African people knew how to mystify the natural resources of the earth for their own benefit, however, because the Europeans didn't understand the connection of African spirituality to mother earth, they started labeling it black magic, and steered Africans away from their own natural power and knowledge. The Europeans would torture the Africans and forbade them from practicing their own natural religion. Mackandal was eventually captured, condemned to death, and burned alive by the French. These are the cruel and uncivilized parts of our history that we must never forget. The brutality of the Europeans against our forefathers creates a false sense of fear to this day because they have no idea when Africans might decide to avenge the cruelty against their ancestors. Mackandal wasn't alone in his quest for freedom that involves African spirituality. Dutty Boukman was another slave from Senegambia (modern-day Senegal and Gambia). He arrived in Haiti from Jamaica and decided immediately he would not remain in captivity any longer. Equipped with his deep knowledge of Vodou, he linked up with Cecile Fatiman, a Vodou Mambo, to preside over the ceremony at Bois Cayiman, which served as the catalyst for the Haitian Revolution in August 1791. Though his involvement in the Haitian Revolution was brief, Boukman became a mystical figure who inspired the revolution to move forward. He was killed in November 1791, briefly after joining the revolution. The French decapitated him after his capture, and paraded his head on a stick around the country, just as the Americans would do 125 years later, when they paraded the head of Charlemagne Peralte as the Caco leader after his capture, during the illegal US invasion of Haiti in 1915. The old racist and imperialist tactics and practices of these Europeans were always to instill fear, and to keep the Africans from revolting. The aura of invincibility displayed by Boukman remains an inspiration for all Haitians to this day.

There were many other African Spiritualists who took part in the Haitian Revolution, including Georges Biassou, a former ally of Toussaint L'Ouverture, who was one of the founding fathers of the Haitian Revolution. Biassou was born in Haiti in 1741 (Saint Domingue, before the island was divided into two separate countries with the Dominican Republic), but fought on the Spanish side when they invaded the Dominican part of Saint Domingue to maintain slavery. After Toussaint L'Ouverture helped the French defeat the Spanish, because the French had made a promise to end slavery on the island, George Biassou moved to St. Augustine, Florida with his family, which was part of the Spanish colony of Cuba at the time, where he became the leader of black militia. He began to build alliances there because he realized the Spanish had tricked him into fighting against his own brothers in Haiti. Georges Biassou remained a loyalist to the Spanish. However, once in Florida, he changed his name to Jorge and provided refuge to the runaway slaves and the planters alike, during the American Revolution. Of course, there's more to the story, but it would take a lifetime to explain the intricacies of the Haitian Revolution, and how the Africans in Haiti outsmarted the French, British, and the Spanish to gain their independence successfully.

STRUGGLING IN
AMERICA

Like most immigrants who are forced to move to the United States illegally, because of imperialist and colonial reinforcement over control of resources, my father faced a lot of hardship on the streets of Miami, when he first landed there. He didn't want to burden my grandparents with his problems, so he took on odd and demeaning jobs to make ends meet. He slept at the YMCA whenever possible and at the homeless shelter whenever a bed was available. There were times when my dad had nowhere to sleep, but he said complaining about it wasn't going to provide him the shelter he needed, so he did what he had to do to keep his spirits up. There was no time to be proud, because his survival depended on how resilient, determined, and focused he had to be during his tribulation. His lowest point would become his highlights later in life. It didn't matter how low he had to bend to make it in the United States on his own, without burdening my grandparents, he wanted to make it against all odds. As far as he was concerned, he didn't knowingly have any family members living in the States that he could lean on. He was focused and determined to figure it all out on his own. My dad took on many humiliating jobs for survival's sake. As long as he could earn enough money to improve his situation, he was fine with any position. No job was beneath or above him. He wanted to create a better situation for himself in the States, so he could change things for my grandparents in Haiti, even though my grandparents hadn't burdened him with anything. Along the way, my dad learned many great lessons, and he stayed humble because he remembered how happy my grandparents have always been with their simple lives. My grandparents were very content with their situation in Haiti. They just wanted better, and much more for their son.

Eventually, my dad managed to save enough money to rent a room from another Haitian comrade in the Little Haiti section of Miami. It wasn't the best situation at the time, but my dad swallowed his pride and made it work. There were many stigmas attached to living in Little Haiti back then. It had never been known as an opulent place until the gentrification that has been taking place lately. It was a breeding ground for all Haitian "just comes," a term used for newly arrived Haitians. Little Haiti is a home community away from home for many Haitian exiles and immigrants in the Miami area. The characterization of the community is obvious upon entry, by its Kreyol and French designations, streets named after Haitian revolutionaries, street life, art galleries, theatre performances on most weekends, dance, music, mom and pop shops, and other family-run enterprises, restaurants and a culture that is uniquely Haitian. Known historically as Lemon City, Little River and Edison, combined, Little Haiti is home to over 27,000 Haitian immigrants and many other residents from other parts of the Caribbean. Soaked in the composite and ornate cultural histories of immigrants from the Caribbean who brought life into the community, Little Haiti has also become a diverse beacon in Miami's art communities. Haitian and other Caribbean talents are in abundance, and art dealers, museums, and other places of exhibit have capitalized on the opportunities. Record stores and other specialty and authentic businesses have eased into the neighborhood, creating a unique practicality found nowhere else in the United States in Haitian communities. The erected statue of General Toussaint L'Ouverture on N. Miami Avenue and 62nd Street alone, the father of the Haitian Revolution, is a daily reminder of home and the great history of Haiti throughout the world. The euphoric feeling in Little Haiti is the antidote for the nostalgic feelings that some Haitians sometimes experience when they think about their homeland. Little Haiti brings a sense of normalcy to many Haitians living in Miami, and to those visiting Haitians from other states, who want to get a sense of home while in Miami. As with any other immigrant groups, Little Haiti wasn't a prime real estate area when it was first founded by Haitian immigrants back in the late 1970's, when over

50,000 Haitians made their way to Miami, while fleeing instability and corruption in Haiti.

My father moved around from one job to another for some time, seeking the best opportunity to earn more money, while simultaneously working multiple jobs to maintain a roof over his head. At night, he would attend classes at the community center to learn English, so he could be proficient enough to move around freely and assimilate into American society with ease. After living in Miami for a couple of years, my dad decided he had had enough. He made up his mind that he wanted to move to New York sooner than later. His ancestors answered his prayers when he was granted his Green card by the Immigration and Naturalization Service department through a lottery system that took place in the state of Florida for immigrants seeking asylum. He had become a permanent resident alien, which gave him full permanent rights and legal status to work and move around throughout America. My dad set out for New York City a week after he received his Green card and never looked back.

My dad didn't get too attached to the people he met in Miami. He had left behind two parents who were getting older and their health was probably becoming more frailty by the day, because they didn't have a full grasp of his circumstances in America, and were worrying daily about him. Though my grandparents put their full trust in their ancestral spirituality, they're still human, so they worried about their son. My grandparents had spent most of their lives trying to provide the best opportunities for my dad. Now, he felt it was his time to repay them. He wanted to do everything in his power to ease the hard work and financial burden off my grandparents. He had also moved to New York City at the urging of an old college colleague from Haiti, whom he had run into in Miami. His colleague convinced him he was way too smart to waste his life working demeaning jobs in Miami, because he could get better opportunities in New York. The man bragged so much when he ran into my father, my dad naively thought he was a major mover and shaker in New York City who could possibly help him land a better job, using his engineering degree. His luck wouldn't change that quickly in New York, though. It wasn't until my father moved to New York City that he discovered the truth about his former colleague. This colleague didn't necessarily graduate from college with my dad in Haiti, but they attended school at the same time. He was a student at the university, but he didn't quite cut it there. The guy's dad, who was a Tonton Macoute at the time, was able to pull some strings to get him admitted into the state university. As far as his educational qualifications, though, that was questionable at best. That was another normalcy that went on in Haiti, where the affluent and influential parents were always able to either buy or influence the admission process at the best schools for their children. The college admission scandal that took place in this country pales in comparisons to what goes on in Haiti. Corruption has no barrier or limit in Haiti.

Anyway, upon arrival in New York, my dad's friend offered him a room for rent in a basement apartment that he shared with his wife in Brooklyn, New York. My dad couldn't believe he had been duped. His colleague was actually working at a public hospital in the custodial department of the City of New York. It seemed more like a career than a job for his friend. He had been at that job since he moved to New York City over 8 years ago. He'd lied to my father to impress him, without realizing they were both facing similar struggles. He finally came clean and told my dad that his current position was the best job he could get at the time, and custodians made good money in New York City, as he put it. Not one to judge his friend because my father's situation was no better, my dad listened cautiously as he planned his next move carefully. He was able to pay his friend three months' rent in advance for the room, so now he only had to worry about getting a job to pay for his food and other necessities. My dad was very preoccupied and driven by success. He'd always been that way. While in Miami, my dad had managed to get his driver's license, but he didn't own a car. He couldn't afford one at the time.

While in Miami, he also looked tirelessly for a job in the engineering field, but no company would hire him, because his college degree wasn't recognized or accepted by the US Department of Education. He felt graduating from college in Haiti was essentially a waste of time, no matter where he was. Things wouldn't be any different in New York City. My father looked for work daily in the engineering field, applying at every place recommended by his friend and other people that he met. Survival was first and foremost, but my dad also worried daily about my grandparents in Haiti. A few weeks after getting rejected by many companies for employment and feeling dejected emotionally by his situation, my dad decided to get his TLC license, so he could work as a cab driver. That was the only way he could earn a decent living quickly at the time, and the best way to accelerate his way out of that room in his friend's basement apartment. His living situation wasn't the best, but he was grateful that his friend had offered to rent him a room. The process to get his TLC license was fairly simple; he had to attend classes and pass a test. My dad became a licensed New York taxi driver in no time.

Back then, there was no GPS to help assist with directions, so my dad had to learn the streets on an actual map to get to his destinations, which was also part of the final exam to get his TLC license in New York. New York City is not easy to navigate, but he mastered it with no problem. However, after he started working, whenever he got lost, things would get a little difficult, if he had to ask the rude people of New York for direction. New York City is not the friendliest city. My father wasn't quite proficient in English yet, when he moved to New York, but his survival skills kicked it whenever necessary. In no time, he was able to learn his way around Manhattan, Brooklyn, and Queens. He mostly picked up fares in Manhattan, and during the slow hours he would make trips to John F Kennedy airport and LaGuardia airport for bigger fares. With more money coming in, my dad was able to partake a little more in the New York Haitian social scene. He never deviated from his roots. He stayed close to his culture and embraced his heritage. My dad limited his social activities to Haitian events, simply because he was more comfortable around his own people and culture, and there was no language barrier that he had to worry about. Imagine how frustrating it is when you can't express yourself in a manner that people can understand or relate to you?

Most immigrants experience a different type of frustration when they move to a new country where they don't know the language. I remember a particular situation that my dad told me about, when, as a baby, I was crying endlessly in the middle of the night, and he couldn't find my pacifier to keep me from crying. According to him, sucking on that pacifier was the only way I could fall asleep. He could differentiate between my cries, and there was also a clear difference when I was hungry and sleepy, and my dad knew it. He had to be at work early in the morning, and I wouldn't stop crying. He told my mother he'd go to the drugstore to pick up a new pacifier for me. However, when my father got to the store, he didn't know the proper name for a "pacifier" in English. He kept asking everyone within earshot in his native tongue, "Can you help me find a "sison" for my daughter?" and nobody at the drugstore knew what that was. Finally, he had to rely on his intellect. He stuck his thumb in his mouth, and said, "My baby's crying, I need the thing babies suck." A clerk at the drugstore finally realized that my dad was looking for a pacifier. That's part of the frustration that some immigrants go through after moving to America when the language is foreign to them. Now, imagine how frustrating it must've been for all of our African ancestors who were purposely and specifically captured from different tribes to keep them from uniting, spoke different languages, and were being taken to a new land in chains, and couldn't even communicate with one another to plan their escape, or discuss their cruel future ahead? Sometimes putting things in their proper perspective is not something that most people do, because our daily functionality is based on the language that we speak collectively. White people removed the collectiveness from Africans from the time they were forced on the slave ships in Africa through the voyage into the New World. A language barrier is also an inhibitor to progress. Their psychological warfare is endless. As black people, we must understand that most of the struggles we continue to face today are rooted in racism. We were inhumanely castrated of all normal functionality as a group. Anyway, when the clerk finally showed my dad where the pacifiers were located, he bought five of them, because he didn't want to go through that humiliation ever again. He also never forgot the word "pacifier," Just as the Cinque character played by Djimon Hounsou, in the movie, Amistad, never forgot the word "Free." For my dad, living in a foreign land was almost like being the only black person in a white neighborhood, there's nothing comfortable about that. My dad enjoyed the comfort of down-home cooking and the free expression of speaking his native tongue to his fellow Haitians and being overall comfortable around only black people.

Soon enough, my dad started meeting new people, and he was able to connect with a woman named Marjorie Etienne. My dad met her through another woman he'd met through another cab driver. This particular woman named Roselyne was a cook who had built her reputation as the best Haitian cook in Brooklyn among all the single Haitian cab drivers in New York City, and all the Haitian cab drivers who were single, without family in New York, used to go to her to purchase their food after work. My dad would go to her house almost every day to pick up a plate of his favorite Haitian food. She had a different menu for every day of the week. She never took time off. She served these men at all hours of the day. These guys were guaranteed a plate of food every day, as long as she was not sick. My dad wanted to stay as connected to his culture as possible, and meeting different Haitian people with diverse backgrounds gave him that opportunity to do just that.

Over time, my dad developed a rapport with the woman who was cooking his food every day, and she took a liking to his character. She became the aunty that he needed in the city where he had no family. They would often talk about his life, her circumstances in New York, and her dreams of one day owning her own restaurant, so they became good friends in no time. She introduced my dad to a cousin of hers named Marjorie that he happened to find very attractive, and was very fond of. In all honesty, Marjorie was a beauty, and my dad just couldn't resist. She was the most beautiful chocolate skinned woman he had ever met, and her gorgeous, inviting smile just melted my dad's heart right away. It also helped that Roselyne was a fan of my dad's character. She thought my dad had great morals, discipline, and drive, which made him perfect for her cousin. While she may have been around a lot of cab drivers, she made it a point to let my dad know that she felt he was different from the rest. She felt my dad had bigger dreams than just being a cab driver. She put in a good word for him with her cousin, and encouraged her to go out on a date with him. My dad was no scrub either. He was a good-looking man, medium brown skinned, standing at 6'ft tall, 180lbs of sexiness and intelligence. Most people think my dad resembled a young Richard Roundtree. That worked in his favor, because Richard Roundtree was a sex symbol to a lot of black women back in the day.

In no time, my dad started going to Roselyne's house, spending more time with her, so that he could see more of Marjorie. He finally worked up the nerve to ask Marjorie out on a date, and she agreed. This was actually the first time my dad had been on a date since he moved to the States. He said he was focused and didn't have time or the money to waste on random women. Haitian culture in general, works differently from other cultures when it comes to dating. It's always easier to date when a person is introduced to the opposite sex by mutual friends, instead of just walking up to someone randomly to make their acquaintance. I guess it establishes a level of trust, familiarity, and a sense of security for both parties. That's definitely not the case for the new generation of Haitians in America today, and that certainly wasn't the case for me and Kane. My dad's first date with Marjorie was a simple dinner and a movie. He said it felt weird that he was driving her on a date in his cab, but the other option was public transportation, because he didn't have a personal car at the time. Marjorie wasn't even bothered by the yellow cab. They talked a lot, and she was smitten by my father's drive and intelligence. She knew there was more to him than just a cab driver. She realized circumstances had forced my dad to take on a job that he didn't necessarily like, because of survival's sake. She saw a lot of potential in him, and she decided she would give him an opportunity to get to know her better.

After a few months of dating and hanging out with Marjorie, my dad felt strong enough that he was in love with her, to propose to her. Of course, Marjorie accepted his proposal, because she felt the same way about him. Their romance didn't seem all that romantic to me whenever I hear the story, but it was a different time and different circumstances for two people who met at a moment when they seemed to have needed one another for security, companionship, and support. They eventually got married and Marjorie would eventually become pregnant with me almost a year into their marriage. Marjorie is the woman who gave birth to me, and who has helped me become the woman that I am today. Her struggles helped her to produce the best child that God could have ever given her. I'm also my mother's only child. I love that woman.

My dad always explained that dating my mom was not about impressing her or buying her expensive gifts that he couldn't afford, but more about the connection they felt when they first started dating. He said back then the family unit was different and black couples leaned on one another more to build stronger family units. The goals were mostly unified and each person did their best to contribute to the family's goals. He said they sat down and discussed their goals in life, and mapped out a plan to achieve that goal together, and those plans included my dad going back to school to earn his engineering degree, and my mom finishing nursing school, so she could become a registered nurse. They also had more children in their plans, but they ended up with just me. The other children never came, but they seem happy with little old me. My mom's strenuous work schedule as a nurse may have played a role in me ending up being an only child, in addition to her developing fibroids in her stomach. I'm not sure if black women are specifically targeted, but this fibroid phenomenon has affected black women the most, and has slowed down the growth of the black population. I'm no conspiracy theorist, but people like Bill Gates scares me, whenever he starts talking about the world being overpopulated, and I know the most marginalized and subjugated group of people are usually the easiest prey. Hopefully, one day black women will discover the true origin of this fibroid phenomenon that has taken control over their bodies. My dad never said whether or not loneliness in a city of eight million people accelerated his decision to ask my mom to marry him, but I also know that sometimes desperate situations call for desperate measures. They must've been truly in love because I can still see it in their eyes to this day. They were two people from different worlds who met on neutral ground in America and fell in love.

However, my mom's situation and journey to America was a little different. She had come to the States on a visitor's visa, and decided to stay here after her visa expired. Though illegal, she managed to work as a nursing assistant to support herself after she decided to stay here. Getting that job as a nursing assistant was an arduous task all on its own because she couldn't legally work in this country. Her goal was to become a registered nurse, but after her visa expired, she was also living in New York illegally, and she couldn't attend school because of that. She never mentioned her immigration status to my dad when they met. She allowed the relationship to take its natural course. I guess the relationship moved to fast between, they decided to get married sooner than later, and the rest is history. Before the actual wedding ceremony, my mom revealed to my dad that her visa had expired, and if she got caught by immigration, she would be deported. She was working through an agency under the table, and the agency owner took advantage of her by paying her less than the other legal nursing assistants she had placed to work in nursing homes across New York City. My mother never complained. She did what she had to do. My dad was more than honored to marry her and, help her file for permanent resident status as his spouse.

Unlike my dad, my mom was born and raised in the capital city of Port-Au-Prince. Since her family was upper middle class, the hurdles she faced back home were not so much. My mom's upper-middle background created many complexes she developed and had to let go after moving to America. There are endless complexities in Haiti that keep Haitian society from thriving, but illiteracy and lack of education for the masses play a major role in that. It wasn't until my mother moved to New York to stay with her cousin, who was cooking food for people in order to survive, that she realized she had better let go of the mentality of the caste system that is practiced in Haiti that most Haitians are completely unaware of. I'm sure it was something adopted from their enslavers over the years, but the freed blacks didn't have time to address it generations ago in Haiti. My mother's father owned a pawn shop, while her mom managed her own grocery store. The two businesses were enough to provide a decent life for my mom and her two siblings, but while growing up, she knew she always wanted more out of life than what my grandparents provided for her. Attending some of the best schools as a child in Haiti throughout her educational life didn't really offer too many benefits that would lead to a career that she wanted in Haiti. My mom was smart enough to recognize how things function in Haiti while she was still in high school. The limitations set on women in Haiti were too obvious to my mother. She knew she couldn't live in a country that treated women as second class citizens, and many women had to rely on men for their survival. Haiti used to be a traditional country where the men went to work as providers, while the women stayed home, but that came with a price at the expense of the wives and unlimited liberty for the husbands to do whatever the hell they wanted. My mom never saw herself living in the shadow of a man, just as her own mother didn't. My grandmother established her own business, while my grandfather ran his business. Even though the majority of street vendors and other small business owners in Haiti are women, Haitian society is male dominated and they have never made it easy for women to be represented in government. The economically disadvantaged women are often exploited by men in powerful positions. Of course, economic duress plays a major role in the misogynistic construct that is so prevalent in Haiti even today. Though my mom didn't see this treatment of women in her immediate family, but it was rampant among the women in her extended family and Haitian society at large. It's a regular practice for men in high positions in Haiti to demand sex from their female subordinates at work, or even before they get hired, in order to secure job positions they are qualified for. My mom would have none of that.

My grandfather raised my mom with a different set of values, and respect for herself was drilled into her mind since she was a toddler. My grandfather was very protective of his family. He made every effort to establish relationships with all the corrupt Tonton Macoutes who lived within the vicinity of their home, and at the same time demanded their respect by also befriending some of the army soldiers who were known as "Leopards," who were also the educated enemies of the Tonton Macoutes. The requirement to become a Tonton Macoute was the ability to breathe, while the requirement to become a member of the special army "Leopards" at a minimum was a high school diploma. Most Tonton Macoutes never set foot in an elementary school, much less graduated from high school, which is why ignorance among them was pervasive. My grandfather knew how to hedge his position. He did favors for many of them whenever they needed to pawn something or borrow money that sometimes they couldn't afford to pay back. It was part of the protection system in Haiti to ensure the safety of his family at all times. My mom grew up with this knowledge and she understood that she would have to compromise her principles in order to live in a society that is so corrupt by government officials. She didn't look down on my father for doing what he had to do to protect his family, but it just wasn't the type of life she saw for herself. As an attractive woman, my mother probably could've thrived in Haiti, or she could've found an affluent man to give her the lifestyle that she wanted, but it probably wouldn't be a man that she loved. A lot of beautiful women in Haiti end up with certain types of men, not because of love, but out of necessity and survival.

It wasn't difficult for my mom to get a visa to visit the States, because my grandparents had demonstrated they had the means to support themselves in Haiti, and they didn't need to move to the US in search of a better life. The US government has certain guidelines in place all over the world to marginalize the poor and to keep them from traveling to the States. There's no access to the American dream, unless an immigrant can demonstrate they have access to their own dream in their homeland. Money plays a major role in obtaining a visa to the United States, which is why poor people often resort to makeshift boats, and long distance journeys on rough terrain on foot to travel to the United States illegally. The barriers for the poor exist worldwide. Most poor people are condemned to poverty for life, without even understanding their life sentence. My mother simply had to show a certain amount of income and savings in the bank, in order to obtain a visa to the United States. In addition, my grandparents knew some people in high places because of my dad's pawn shop, and were able to grease a few hands to get my mom a visitor's visa to the US without any problem. It was supposed to be a brief vacation to America and nothing more. However, my mom never told her parents she never intended to come back to Haiti. From the very beginning, she had planned on staying in the US indefinitely during her visit. She didn't put much thought into changing her legal status to a permanent resident, but she was determined not to go back to Haiti, because she didn't want to end up with a life she didn't establish for herself on her own. My mother was temporarily staying with one of my grandfather's cousins the first couple of weeks when she first arrived in New York. Things were good at first, until she mentioned to her cousin she was planning to stay permanently in the States. Her cousin had always secretly harbored animosity toward her parents back in Haiti for having managed to create a decent life for themselves and their children. In America, this cousin felt the playing fields were leveled, and he even had some leverage because he had been in New York for a while and had established himself. That animosity would manifest itself months later when her cousin tried to force himself on my mom, her own blood cousin. That was the end of their relationship and her stay at her cousin's house.

My mom lived her best life in Haiti, and even was able to vacation in the Dominican Republic, the Bahamas, Panama, and Venezuela with my grandparents at times, a luxury her extended family members never could enjoy, due to financial restraints. However, her parents never looked down on other family members. As a matter of fact, they helped as much as they could whenever possible. Her cousin crossing the line trying to sleep with her was unacceptable. My mom was not destitute, as she put it. She came to New York with enough pocket money to last her just the month she had told my grandparents she was coming to New York to stay for, but after she decided to extend her stay, her money was running short, and she had a hard time mustering the courage to reach out to my grandparents to ask them to send her more money. They were expecting her return within a month. My mother's future was the family business, but the family business wasn't in my mom's plans. She had to get away from my grandparents to make decisions for herself, because Haitian culture allows the parents to have dominance over their children for as long as the children live with them, or as long as they think they can run their children's lives. At first, my mom's cousin told her not to worry about anything, and that he would help her any way he could. She trusted him, and thought life in New York was eventually going to become easier for her. She was wrong. She should've read all the wrong signals coming from her cousin in the very beginning.

When she first arrived, her cousin was living in a 2-room basement apartment with a small kitchen. He slept on the couch for the first week she was there, while she slept in the small bedroom. Everything was going great at first. He took her out and showed her as many places in New York as possible, whenever he was off work. My mom was a very attractive woman, so of course, she was getting a lot of attention from different men. It wasn't until she met this young man who took a liking to her, that her cousin started to act jealous, and started showing his animosity toward her and her family. One thing led to another, my mom found herself almost on the street with nowhere to live, and she had to swallow her pride and called her parents to send her money to rent a room in a rooming house. Her cousin decided to ruin his blood kinship to my mom when he attempted to force himself on her sexually one night. She ran out the door, and called her friend whom she had been casually dating, to pick her up. He was an old pubescent boyfriend she had in Haiti, and they had kept in touch after he had moved to the States five years earlier. The biggest physical interaction between them back in Haiti was holding hands. It would be the same thing all over again a few months after my mom left her cousin's house, when her new beau decided he wanted to have sex with her as well, even though she wasn't ready, willing, or emotionally wanting to have sex with him. Sex was always sacred to my mom, and there was a psychological component attached to it, because she had seen the women in her extended family in Haiti forced into compromising sexual positions with men, for their survival. She didn't want her first sexual experience to be with someone she wasn't in love with, and didn't want a man who wasn't compassionate enough to understand that she wanted her first sexual experience to be special. Tears welled up in my mom's eyes when she was telling me the story, and I cried right along with her. The funny thing about the situation is that she actually liked him. All she wanted was for him to wait a little while, until she was ready. After that incident, she realized that young man definitely wasn't the man for her. He tried to force her to have sexual relations with him after just a few weeks after my mom started staying with him. She realized that not too many men were willing to play the waiting game. Patience is a virtue.

Whenever I heard these stories from my immigrant parents, I realized how lucky I am to have parents who sacrificed so much to provide a better life for me and protect me for most of my life. When my mom decided to leave her friend's house that night, she reached out to another cousin on her mother's side of the family. And that woman was the sweetest person that my mom could've ever encountered in New York. Roselyne came over with a friend right away to pick up my mom to take her to her house. At the time Roslyn was living in a two-bedroom apartment with her 2 children. Thank goodness for Haitian customs, because she invited my mother to sleep in the bed with her. Haitian families have no problem sharing the bed with other family members of the same sex. Cousins usually sleep together with no problem, even as adults. There's nothing taboo about it. It's family. My mom ended up staying with her cousin Roselyne who helped her the best way she could, until she met my dad.

My mom was destined to meet Jean Francois, my dad, and he was destined to meet Marjorie, my mom, which brought the conception of Candace, which is I. My dad and my mom consummated their relationship once they both felt comfortable and ready before they got married. However, it wasn't until a few months into their honeymoon period as a new couple that I was conceived. Both my parents had faced arduous adversities as young immigrants in America, but they both managed to persevere, and both eventually ended up achieving their American dreams. My dad went back to school through an adult education evening program offered at the City College of New York and became a civil engineer and my mom worked her ass off at night and attended nursing school during the day to become a registered nurse. At first, it was hard on their relationship, but they made the sacrifices and compromised for their relationship to work. If nothing at all, as their child, I was their motivation to stay focused and achieve their goals. I have been a prized child to my parents since birth. My dad protected me the best way that he could, but most of all, he instilled values in me that always kept me from compromising my integrity. My mom always pointed to my dad as a great example of the type of character that I should look for in a man. Kane was definitely that man. I just hoped that my parents would eventually grow to love him like he was their own son.

CANDACE'S UPBRINGING

Education is vast, according to my dad, and he had never set limits on me, as far as educating myself. He wanted me to absorb as much information as possible, just like he did. He'd always made it a priority to teach me about the politics of the world, especially American politics and policies, and how they affect the rest of the world. My father was very aware of the obstacles and adversities thrown in the path of his home country of Haiti, by the United States, France, and Canada. He has also taught me that these imperialists had been throwing rocks at Haiti and hiding their hands for years, ever since Haiti became the first free black republic in the western hemisphere. The US has always been an arch enemy of Haiti, simply because of the threat that Haiti's independence posed to their slavery system in America. They have been determined for years now to destroy Haiti by all means. They've been shining the spotlight on Haiti forever, while hiding the fact that they received a lot of help from the Haitian people before America became a first world. Without the Haitian revolution, Napoleon's army wouldn't have been exhausted and bankrupt to the point where the US was able to exercise the Louisiana Purchase which extended to Arkansas, Kansas, Missouri, Iowa, North and South Dakota, Nebraska, and Oklahoma for just a million dollars. That purchas stretched America to a third larger of its original size, thanks to the Haitian Revolution, but they don't teach young Americans that the Haitian Revolution played a major role in helping America to expand its territory by almost forty percent.

The false philanthropic narrative about sending aid to Haiti and other third-world nations is just to propagate a fallacy that the US is the leader of the world. The US has limited natural resources, which ultimately means their currency is worthless. For every dollar this government gives to another "third world nation" in aid, they usually walk away with a hundred dollars in resources. Haiti is vastly resourceful. My father made it clear to me that most of the third world nations around the world are created by the white imperialist nations that have labeled them as such, through exploitation of their resources and labor. There are few countries in the Caribbean and Africa without enough natural resources to sustain their own population and economy. However, these greedy colonizing countries usually through forced embargoes and cooperative measures, always concoct plans to steal the much needed resources away from these nations, and then turn around to call them poor. My father schooled me on many things while growing up, but the one thing he reinforced all the time was the fact that America has forced many people to migrate to their shores, because they refuse to keep their dirty and greedy paws off people's natural resources, properties, and labor force. To the dismay of many immigrants from around the world who live here and in other "developed countries," they are often forced to flee their home country to migrate to other foreign countries in search of a better life, because of outside intervention from the international imperialist nations that set out to exploit them. Still, few people, especially Americans, understand the role that America and the other colonizers cohesively play in destabilizing countries politically and economically around the world.

While teaching me about his own personal history back home in Haiti, my father never failed to mention that the United States was the biggest benefactor of Papa Doc Duvalier and Baby Doc's reign in Haiti. One of the things that I enjoyed as a little girl, were the assignments my dad would allot to me, which kept me busy whenever we were at the library together. Learning everything about Haitian history was the most popular assignment that I received from my dad. He wanted to drill into my head the important role that Haiti played in ending slavery around the world. I learned through my research, the dirty tactics that the United States government used to undermine the Haitian economy and Haitian society as a whole since 1915. At one point, they made it their mission to convince or coerce the Haitian government into changing the country's economic disposition from agricultural to industrial. As is normally done by white imperialists looking for their best interest in black people and black countries around the world, America forced an industrial revolution down Haiti's throats, while completely annihilating Haiti's self-dependency on agriculture. The industrial revolution only benefitted the United States government and American businesses, as Haiti became a plantation for cheap labor, handicapped by her inability to produce anything for her own people, while the Dominican Republic developed agriculturally to help sustain the needs of their Haitian neighbor. The destruction of the Haitian agricultural economy forced the exodus of many Haitian planters to the Dominican Republic. Of course, the Dominican Republic had long succumbed to US pressure to become a hub for US companies, but the deal between Haiti and the US also brought a different type of prosperity to the Dominican Republic, which destroyed Haiti's economy and livelihood in the process. While the United States government was tooting its own horn about being the defender of human rights around the world, under the auspices of the world's leading nation, they were forcing Haitians to work for slave wages, and manipulating the economy of Haiti, in order to boost the economy of the Dominican Republic, their unofficial territory.

It's not a coincidence that America invaded Haiti in 1915, because it was a thriving black nation. A few years after the invasion of Haiti, America would repeat history on its own soil by destroying the Greenwood section of Tulsa, Oklahoma, better know as Black Wall Street, six years later on May 31ˢᵗ through June 1ˢᵗ in 1921, because white people have a problem with black progress, even when it's their own black citizens. It was the first time in history the US government bombed it's own city. It wasn't just the racists who wanted to see the demise of black people, but also the US government, which has refused to allow black people to thrive in this nation, or anywhere in the world.

My dad had always told me to be careful of white people, because oftentimes their good intentions are only good for them, and only benefit them, as was the case in Haiti when American companies promised to bring jobs to Haiti, once Haiti became industrialized. What ended up happening was a slew of US factories were created and Haitians were forced to work for slave wages that couldn't even afford them the luxury of a decent meal daily. As late as 2009, Hillary Clinton continued to fight on behalf of the United States government in Haiti to make sure wages paid by American companies to Haitians were below the poverty line. When Haitian leaders disagreed with her, she threatened them with embargoes and vowed vengeance by the United States government. It was extortion at its best. Bill Clinton falsely professed his love for Haiti as a tactic to gain the confidence of Haitian leaders and support from the Haitian people in the Diaspora. A con artist in plain sight and a wolf in sheep's clothing, Bill Clinton has always looked for his own self-interest in Haiti, and was able to con Haitians, the same way he conned African-Americans in America to support him when he ran for president, with his phony saxophone theatrics on the Arsenio Hall show. Hillary Clinton, while working for the Obama administration as Secretary of State, worked in cahoots with US corporations, including Hanes, Levi's, Fruit of the Looms, and many others, to keep Haitian factory workers from getting an increase in pay from .24 cents an hour to .61 cents an hour.

While the US media likes to label Haiti the poorest country in the western hemisphere, we must question why they continue to fight the Haitian government whenever they ask for livable wages for Haitian workers who work in American factories in Haiti. As with all things beneficial to white people, as it relates to black people, the Clintons were also the first people to land in Haiti after the catastrophic earthquake that killed over 300,000 people on January 12, 2010. The Clintons were there to simply loot the country's riches, the collected donations through their foundation, and nothing more. Through their shell companies and the Clinton Foundation, the Clintons used their influence as fake ambassadors on behalf of Haiti to further marginalize and subjugate the people of Haiti. These 2 devils should never be welcomed in Haiti, as they are adversaries, not allies of the Haitian people. This is fact! My father can't stand the Clintons, and if there were any justice in this world, Hillary and Bill Clinton would be rotting in a jail cell until they fucking die. America has always been endemic to Haiti. After Haitians successfully defeated the French in Haiti to gain their independence, America refused to recognize Haiti as an independent republic, unless Haiti paid an extortion fee to France for having valiantly defeated them. Haiti was forced into a corner, because they had no access to world trade.

According to my dad through his own research and homework about Haiti, Haitians have been paying the price for debunking white supremacy and white superiority for over a century now, and many white chameleons have acted like friends of Haiti, while working closely with Haitian officials to figure out ways to keep Haiti in a cycle of poverty and to completely condemn the first free black nation in the world to chaos and instability. This is what I've learned: As most thieves would do before breaking into a home, they would always make sure they do their homework to ensure there are valuables to be stolen before breaking in, and the Clintons did exactly that in Haiti. They were well aware of the amount of money that was going to be poured into Haiti after the 2010 earthquake, and they positioned themselves to rob the country of the opportunity to rebuild itself as the Pearl of the Antilles. The earthquake in Haiti offered them the perfect camouflage to come in as philanthropists and fake ambassadors, while exploring Haiti's natural resources and riches. The iridium, oil, and gold found in Haiti are worth trillions of dollars, and America set out to take it all, while proclaiming on their national television and other media outlets that Haiti is the poorest nation in the world every day. The false narrative about Haiti being a poor country, or any other African nation for that matter, is constituted upon the theft of those natural resources by "developed countries," such as America, France, and England that have extorted Africa and the Caribbean to the tune of a trillion dollars annually. There isn't one poor country in Africa, and Haiti is not poor, due to the unlimited natural resources possessed by these countries. However, the colonizers of the world love to use their fake goodwill as a veil to rob these countries of their resources, while pushing propaganda and selling the false narrative that these countries are poor. Africa and the Caribbean have supported the lifestyle of white people around the world since slavery. I would've bought into their false propaganda, if my father wasn't such an intelligent man who educated me well on his country of birth, and the history of these enslavers and imperialists around the world. I will always be proud of my Haitian heritage and African ancestry, as Haiti will once again rise from the ashes, and Africa will become the leading continent in the world.

Showing pride in my heritage has always been a priority for my dad. "I want you to walk in the world with your head high, because you have a rich history, despite what the world may be saying about

Haitians. And remember, before the Haitian nationality was forced upon your great great grandparents, they were Africans first. I want you to always be proud of your African and Haitian heritage. Don't ever allow anybody to diminish the accomplishments of your ancestors. They stood up and fought evil, and they won," my dad would tell me when I was a little girl. As an adult, I have a better grasp of the values my dad was trying to instill in me. My American nationality doesn't define me as an African and Haitian woman. Too many people get caught up in the pride of their place of birth. Black people are responsible for the world's economy, because slavery was a major part of the development of most of the developed and leading countries in the world today, in addition to the trillions stolen in African resources annually. I'm well aware of my history and their lies against my people. I plan on fortifying the minds of my children with their true history, the same way my dad was able to fortify my mind.

KANE'S GRANDPARENTS' INFLUENCE ON HIM

The more I listened to Candace's family story, the more I realized we had so much in common as a black couple, with vastly different backgrounds. While her parents may have moved from Haiti to escape poverty, marginalization, exploitation, oppression, subjugation, and so many other dire circumstances forced upon them by the United States, France, Canada, and other imperialist nations that refused to allow Haiti to thrive as an independent nation, my grandparents did the same exact thing here in America when they moved from the south to the north, to escape Jim Crow laws, poverty, lack of opportunity and racism, while in search of a better life for their children. The tactics the US government has used to keep Haiti from thriving are the same tactics they have used against black people in America for the last couple of centuries. Through my research, I've learned the World Bank and the IMF (The International Monetary Fund) also play a major role in marginalizing so-called "Third World countries." These "Third World countries" usually have their money stolen, resources exploited, and cheap labor forced upon their people by countries like the United States, France, and Britain, in order to develop themselves as first world nations. The World Bank and the IMF have a specific clause in their lending agreement that prevents third world countries whose resources have been stolen by developed countries, from nationalizing their resources, which means that white people and white companies can come at any time to steal their resources whenever they want, if they're not nationalized. In addition, money from the World Bank and the IMF usually ends up back in the hands of the imperialist contractors.

History is one of my favorite subjects, and I'm always willing to share it with anyone who would listen. I acquired some knowledge about Haiti after I met Candace. I wanted to know more about her culture, so I read as many books as I could about Haiti as the first black republic, and the resilience of the Haitian people to defeat the French and end slavery, not just in Haiti, but also helping to end slavery in the entire New World. When the US colonizers illegally invaded Haiti in 1915, they looted everything they could find, including Haiti's money, which they moved to Citi Bank illegally, and they stole Haiti's gold reserves. Black progress has always been a threat to white reality, white theft, white lies, and the false history written in the history books to elevate white people, while denigrating black people in the most inferior ways, in order to create a false sense of superiority and supremacy among white people worldwide. White supremacy cannot thrive without deception, destruction of others, and the undermining of black people and black progress, dating all the way back to 1619 in America, which is why Black Wall Street in Tulsa, Oklahoma, Rosewood in Florida, and so many other thriving black towns and cities across the country were destroyed by them. They cannot stand the fact that black people are so resilient, that our spirit is not easily broken.

The false narrative that black people are less intelligent than them is what they have used to force poor white people to harbor hatred toward black people, to make white people feel superior, and to keep the division among the races. Even though the majority of welfare recipients are white people, and the majority of crimes are committed by white people in this country, the media continues to propagate a different narrative, in order to inspire white supremacy. Lyndon B. Johnson was quoted as saying, "If you can convince the lowest white man he's better than the best colored man, he won't notice you're picking his pocket. Hell, give him somebody to look down on, and he'll empty his pockets for you." Even though it was an off-the-cuff observation by Johnson, that statement is rooted in his own upbringing around racist whites in the South, and the values that were instilled in him. To this day, the media cannot let go of the lie that there are more black people in prison than white people.

How can that be? According to the publicly recorded stats, there are roughly 1,200,000 people in all the prison systems in America, from local, state, to the federal level. Of that number, 57 percent of incarcerated people around the country are white, which amounts to 684,000 people. It's not even mathematically possible for black people to exceed the number of people incarcerated in this country, because only 38 percent of people incarcerated in this country are black, which amounts to 456,000. However, the media usually flips the stats in white people's favor by linking the total percentage of black people in the US, to point out that we are greater in numbers mathematically in prison. Of course, I won't even address the fact that black people are ten times more likely to be targeted and pro-filed by police than white people, and it's been proven that many of those black people in prison are innocent, and have been set up, because of systemic racism.

I'm no historian, but I've done my fair share of reading about the history of this country to know the endless role the US govern-ment has played in making sure that black people are oppressed, exploited, marginalized, and subjugated. If they can go that far to make sure their own black citizens are limited in every capacity, I can only imagine what they would do to black people from for-eign countries to keep them thriving. While white people often see fewer convictions in the criminal courts because of white privilege, it doesn't mean they have a lower tendency to act criminally than black people. The majority of murders, rapes, robberies, and other serious crimes are committed by white people, but the media is being used as a propaganda machine to convince the world that black people lead in all criminal categories and activities. In repeating this on every media platform and outlet, they want you to believe that they are concrete with their facts. As a matter of fact, here's the concrete fact about the prison system in America; it outsources prison labor to most of America's corporations, which is why America has the highest number of incarcerated people in the world. Slavery with any other name would be an embellishment.

Some white people even have the audacity to call black people lazy, even though their forefathers' lazy asses went all the way across Africa to kidnap black people to bring to America, the Caribbean, South, and Central America, to do the work their lazy asses refused to do. I was also well-schooled by my grandfather in the history of slavery in this country. My grandfather started to develop an appetite for reading and knowledge as an adult because he didn't have the opportunity to attend school like a normal child. He had to help take care of his sibling as the eldest child in his family. He quit school in the 7th grade to help his parents harvest cotton. It wasn't until after my grandfather moved to Boston that he decided to attend night school to earn his GED. However, once he started quenching his thirst for knowledge, nothing could get in his way, and I ended up being the beneficiary of all that he learned. He was especially interested in the history of Africa, and he read every book he could find about the history of black people around the world, including the slave trade, the Haitian Revolution, and the many different slave revolts that took place in the United States. My grandfather is a wealth of knowledge.

To fathom the idea that black people can intellectually be on par with white people is to conceive a threat to their existence, livelihood and their false sense of superiority and their need to act as "saviors" across the world. Even when some black people have managed to carve better lives for themselves, white people still find a way to resist their progress because of jealousy and envy. I understand that a lot of people have seen some of the desperate measures that some black and brown people have taken to come to America, but few people understand the reason behind their desperation.

America has forced poverty upon people worldwide, but especially upon black and brown countries. I just know if somebody came to my house and stole my television, my refrigerator, my stove, and all the food in my pantry, I would have no choice but to show up at their house to see if I can watch television and to find something to eat. America has extorted as many countries as they can, as it relates to resources, and used their extortion as a means to demean those countries publicly and humiliate the citizens of those countries when they show up on US borders or shores. America has made it so difficult for other countries to be self-sufficient because even when they straight out steal a country's resources, they undermine their economy in other ways through embargoes that they cohesively work with trading partners to enforce. A lot of people in so-called third world nations have no choice but to leave their home country to find a better life in America. I liken the action of the immigrants who come to America to what Henry "Box" Brown had to do in 1849 in Virginia. He felt so desperate to get away from those Jim Crow laws in the South, he placed himself in a wooden crate and had himself shipped to Philadelphia to escape to a city where slavery was illegal, and joined the abolitionists who could provide him with the protection he needed from his oppressor. Forced poverty is no different than forced slavery. It was a clever and desperate move at the same time, because Henry Brown had no idea whether or not he was going make it to Philadelphia safely, and what awaited him during the journey to Philadelphia. It was a risk he was willing to take, because it was worth leaving the existing situation that he no longer wanted to subject himself to. When some of these immigrants decide to make their way to the United States, they are chasing a dream, even though there's no guarantee and most of them may not even make it to their destination.

The United States has sold itself to the world as the land of milk and honey, but where is their milk and honey coming from? Who's left starving so they can have so much milk and honey? We can't keep judging people without walking a mile in their shoes. Since

I was a child in Boston, I've noticed these racists in America and other imperialist nations around the world have purposely created campaigns to promote Haitian phobia for many years, but nobody has questioned their tactics. I've only been paying closer attention to this matter because the love of my life is Haitian. Prior to meeting Candace, I probably thought the way that most Americans were thinking, and that was my lack of sympathy, empathy, knowledge, education, and comprehension as to why some people were willing to leave their home country, to sacrifice their safety, without knowing what awaited them. This government had unjustly blamed HIV and AIDS on Haitians for years, when there has never been any absolute evidence to support their false claims and arguments dating back to the early 80's, and they've purposely and continuously kept their campaign about Haiti relevant with each new administration. Even my own mother had made an ignorant comment regarding AIDS, as it relates to Candace. I had to check her on it, and educate her at the same time.

The most ignorant and outspoken president of all time, Donald Trump, couldn't keep his racist mouth shut about Haiti. He even referred to Haiti as a shithole country. That's to reaffirm that they are going to completely strip Haiti of its history for having brought white supremacy to its knees during the Haitian Revolution. Disparaging Haiti has been the order of every administration, so that people can no longer use Haiti's great history as a reference for black liberation around the world. One has to question the motive behind the US government constantly reminding the world that Haiti is the poorest country in the western hemisphere, yet, they have their second largest US embassy in the world located in Haiti. It got me thinking about the fact that Trump has never set foot in Haiti, but felt qualified to make disparaging comments about Haiti. The shithole he referred to could very well be the shit he has for brains or his shitty breath. Who knows? When this government forces you to focus and hate on a specific group of people, in due time, you won't care what happens to them or how they are treated in society, and all your sensibilities toward them will disappear. They have managed to do the same thing to black people in this country. People in this country are now so desensitized to the killing of black men at the hands of police officers, because the imagery has been normalized on all media platforms, and most of the time, these police officers aren't even indicted after unjustly killing a black person. It is a tactic that has been perfected through practice, propaganda, and false narratives told by the media. As a matter of fact, I realized that they can easily turn anybody into a culprit for anything through their false propaganda machine which is the media, but a person must be hip to their game to see through their bullshit tactics of assassinating the character of the victims posthumously and vilifying them in death. They've done this to black people in America for so long, that few black folks are even aware of this endless campaign here and across the world to create black phobia and vilify black people. How can you fear a group of people that you managed to enslave on a global scale? It's a psychological game that white people have used to gain approval worldwide over the way they treat black people.

My grandmothers and grandfathers, from both, my paternal and maternal sides, are from the south. My paternal grandparents are from Hayti, North Carolina, also known as modern day Durham, NBorth Carolina, while my maternal grandparents are from LaGrange, Georgia. As a kid, I heard the stories from my grandparents about the freedmen in North Carolina establishing Hayti as a city after the Civil War, in honor of the Haitian Revolution. I'd also heard about the maltreatment of black people in the 1940's and 1950's in the south. A lot of the 93 cities established by Freedmen across the country were purposely destroyed, and black people had to start all over again, without any compensation from the government for the destruction. Jim Crow laws prevented black people from doing many things, or becoming anything in life, and their lives were always in danger because the Ku Klux Klan in the South endlessly used intimidation tactics to scare and hurt black people. The records do not truly reflect the number of black people who have been murdered in the South by the Ku Klux Klan. According to my grandparents, many of their murder victims went unreported, and most of these killings were committed by racist officers who worked for the police and sheriff departments locally.

They felt powerless and never felt completely free as American citizens, because there were so many restrictions to black mobility and progress in the South. Jim Crow laws and the Confederacy were, and probably still are part of the identity of the South. My grandparents were also trying to escape the grips of poverty and their dire circumstances, when they decided to move up north to Boston to establish themselves. There were limited opportunities for black people in the South as far as employment, and many black people continued to pick cotton for unlivable wages at the time, just to survive.

The Emancipation Proclamation didn't exactly free anybody. It empowered the South in a different way with the emergence of Jim Crow laws, which were created to limit the movement of black people and to criminalize them as freemen and women with nowhere to go. Vagrancy laws on the books were purposely established to further marginalize and subjugate black folk. These laws took black people from the plantation of white private owners, to the state and federally-owned prisons where their labor was still outsourced to support slavery and the plantation owners at a discounted rate. This practice, unfortunately, continues to this day and is masked in so many different neo-colonialist ways, that black people no longer recognize their own exploitation. As the first black president of this country, Obama failed black people miserably. He failed us in the sense that he was more concerned about gay rights, than he was about ratifying the 13th amendment to completely ban slavery, by eradicating the exception that makes slavery legal as long as a person is incarcerated.

Though the Civil Rights Act of 1965 banned pay discrimination on the basis of race, black men and women continue to earn less than their white counterparts in all facets of professional industries. Black college graduates earn just about as much as white high school graduates today, which further extends the racial wage gap between black and white people. While black people were told that they needed more education in order to climb the ladder at work, inevitably racism trumps everything and college educated black men still earn less than high school educated white men. For black women, the disparity is even bigger, even though black women have become the most educated group in this country. In addition to the disparity in pay, black college graduates are crippled with student loans that they have to repay, which often prevents them from qualifying for a mortgage. Home-ownership is the gateway to wealth, but the roadblocks, hurdles, and adversities tend to pile up on the path of black folks. Racism is injustice on every level for black people. Equality in the workplace is not truly practiced, and has never existed in America for black people.

The Civil Rights Act has been used as a smokescreen to keep black folks from bringing attention to the issues affecting them. In other words, it was a pacifier that eventually became a muzzle. I'm not one to believe in their analytics all the time, but black men earn a disappointing .87 cents for every dollar white men earn doing the exact same job. To further support modern day slavery, Bill Clinton, as president signed into law the Mass Incarceration legislation that Biden had been fighting for since President Ronald Reagan was in office, cementing the faith of black families. It was the beginning of the decimation of the black family. Millions of black men were unjustly incarcerated, which destroyed a significant portion of the black family unit, and disintegrated their wealth throughout the 90's.

Black prisoners were contracted by America's biggest corporations while behind bars to work for pennies on the dollar per hour. Fake public apologies from racist politicians posthumously can't undo the damage they have caused to the black community. Black folks are often forced into a position of "forgive and forget," because a lot of black puppets are still looking to build careers off the backs and struggles of black people for a piece of the pie, and white politicians usually know how to identify these puppets for exploitation. There has never been a greater black puppet in history than former president Barack Obama. It's very easy to use the Ivy League educated Negro against his own people, because black people are often overjoyed with symbolic victories and achievements they feel are not attainable by common black folk. The coursework at Harvard University is no more stringent than the coursework at

Howard University or Spellman College, but white supremacy had established guidelines long ago that set them apart as Ivy League schools, even when though those guidelines are based on nepotism than merit. Black people have always excelled at these Ivy League schools. There's truly no prestige attached to all the things white people call prestigious. Cecil Rhodes was a murderer and scumbag, but being a Rhodes Scholar is considered prestigious. Even when apartheid played a major role in sports, white people were lying to the world that they were athletically superior, until black people were given access and started to obliterate the records set by the so-called superior white athletes in every sport. I learned so much from my grandparents who weren't the most educated people that I had been around, but they were the smartest folks I knew. My grandfather recommended many books to me, and he always told me that they can never enslave the minds of people who seek education outside of their realm.

Of course, my paternal grandfather was the eldest in his family, so he had to go to Boston first, and make his own way, in order to establish himself, before he could send for his other siblings. Back then, black folks used to migrate to the North almost one at a time. One family member would move up north, and once established, he/she would send for another family member, until the entire family was relocated. Black people in Africa and the Caribbean also do the same thing, I learned from Candace. The migration might've been within the United States, but my grandparents' stories were very similar to that of Candace's family. Back in the 50s and 60s, black people didn't really separate themselves or fight over nationality as much as they do today. They formed a collective to fight for their civil rights as a unit in this country. My granddaddy used to tell me the stories of visionary leaders like Marcus Garvey who created a Pan-African movement to change the outlook for black people of all backgrounds, even though he emigrated from Jamaica. His vision for black folks to return to Africa was embraced by most black people in America. Black people unified for one common goal, which was the advancement of all black people, liberty, and equality for all black folks. Mr. Garvey, as a Pan-Africanist, fought to unite all black people, and wanted to see the return of all black people to Africa for a better prosperous life. W.E.B. DuBois was the one person who opposed Mr. Marcus Garvey's movement the most, but he soon realized he had been used by the government to become a traitor to his own race and an agent against Mr. Garvey's movement, which could've benefitted a lot of black people. Since he was a staunch opponent of the movement, the system used him to discredit Mr. Garvey with the black elite, and to make sure black people fell in line. Ironically, W.E.B DuBois ended up moving to Ghana and lived there until his death. The United States was not, and has never been ready for a mass exodus of black people. The black labor force and black ingenuity are needed in America, in order for this country to thrive and maintain its position as the leading economy in the world, my grandfather told me.

My grandparents encountered a lot of people from the West Indies after they first moved to Boston, and they became friends with many of them, while living in the Roxbury section of Boston when they first got there. Roxbury used to be the Mecca for black folks in Boston back in the 40's, 50's and 60's. Don't be fooled by all the gentrification that has taken place in Roxbury recently. Black people have been pushed out, as they are in every major urban hub across America. A man from Trinidad who lived in Roxbury, in fact, rented my grandfather a room after he arrived in Boston. That man also helped him land a job at the Park Plaza Hotel as a skycap. Jobs like skycaps, porters on the trains, and other subservient positions were always available to black people, especially in Boston. The great migration didn't only include Boston. Black people in the South were fleeing to New York City, Philadelphia, Chicago, Los Angeles, Detroit, and many other cities that offered them better employment opportunities, and places where Jim Crow laws weren't as prevalent. However, somewhere along the way, the great divide among black people started to take place. Immigrants, not just black ones, but also Asians, Hispanics, and whites, from other countries, were moving into communities that were already established here for black people, by black people. Of course, there was resentment, and justifiably so, over the sharing of resources and the differences in cultures, coupled with the fact that white society had always created a wedge between African and Caribbean blacks, other immigrants, and native blacks. My grandfather was a veteran of World War II, so he knew how to navigate the waters. His hope was to get a job at the Charlestown Navy Yard, but he had to settle for the job at the Park Plaza Hotel when the position at the Navy Yard didn't materialize. Until his death, he never forgot all the assistance his Trinidadian friend provided to him. My grandparents were brave enough to make the decision to move to an entirely new city, just so they could create a better life for their families, which is why I have a lot of respect for most immigrants, but especially the black immigrants who forgo their fear of leaving their home country to subject themselves to racism for the benefit of their family in this country. This country is already hell for African-Americans, but most black immigrants have been sold on a false narrative that this is the land of opportunity, because opportunities have been removed from their homeland by America and its imperialist European allies.

The US media has always done a great job placing a target on the backs of black people, in order to cultivate a form of marginalization and subjugation that ensures black culpability, even though black people are already suffering in every aspect of life here. The use of false narratives and propaganda to reinforce stereotypes about black people has worked to perfection, because so many black people have failed to question the motives behind it. The media conglomerates are owned by 9 corporations, and these conglomerates are the conduit that work together to basically create the false propaganda that grows into false narratives they subject black people to, and homogenize us as a group in everything that we do, in spite of our differences in education, life experience, upbringing, culture and so on. Sensationalizing white supremacy helps motivate white people to be against people who are nonwhite. We see there's always a great white hope in every sport that is created through false narratives, only for those people to fall victim to their own athletic inferiority and not live up to the hype, because they lack the physical superiority, talent, and natural athletic gift of black athletes, most of the time.

White sensationalism keeps this country moving forward, and people like Tucker Carlson and every other media personality and fake journalist on Fox News take advantage of this ignorance. White superiority is a selling point on the news, the movies, and social media, which creates white saviors. Where else can we find a white samurai in Japan played by Tom Cruise, or a white Tarzan who's better equipped to deal with animals in the jungles of Africa, a place that white people are not indigenous to? Not to mention, the many other characters that have been whitened in film history to promote white supremacy. The social engineering of the mind is administered through television, the movies, and now through social media. Social media platforms are quick to banish truth speakers. Most people have their eyes closed to the obvious tampering of their true reality in the world, because they have managed to create a falsehood that has become believable, even to the people they're lying about. This mind-altering drug called white supremacy is the most dangerous drug that the world has seen. Across the world, people have heard false narratives and stereotypes about black people in America, even before setting foot on American soil, or much less, coming into contact with an African-American. Most West Indians and other black people from Africa who move here usually don't understand the power structure, the adversities, and the obstacles that keep African-Americans in a hopeless position when they arrive here. The reason for this, is most black folks from the Caribbean and Africa are marginalized, subjugated, oppressed, and exploited from a distance by the colonizers. In addition, the corrupt black faces that are imposed on them as presidents or prime ministers to secure the interests of white imperialism, keep them in the dark about their own impossibilities at home, and they are usually ruled with punitive violence. Though corruption is rampant across Africa and the Caribbean, the populace are usually unaware of the global puppetry involved, and the threat looming over the life of the imposed/sitting puppets, should they decided not to play the West's games to make sure white imperialism benefit from their natural resources anymore. Still, in due time, most of the black immigrants who move here often learn quickly enough how their African or West Indian heritage doesn't shield them from the same systemic racist treatment that African-Americans have received at the hands of white people. Assimilation into American society for all black immigrants is limited to African-American culture, whether they like it or not. No matter how much a black immigrant would like to adopt white culture, there's a roadblock called racism that will wake them out of their stupor. Of course, many immigrants have tried their best to stay away from African-Americans, even their own kind, once they gain access to white people. They sometimes become interracially involved and all of a sudden start to find faults with their own culture and people. The whitewashing of their minds sometimes prevents them from developing a sense of reality about racism.

The unfortunate part of African and Caribbean marginalization is that it takes place from afar, without direct daily contact and interaction with white people. Africans and West Indian people tend to believe they are not as marginalized as African-Americans, because they don't wake up every day in a world crowded with white people. However, most of the countries that I've traveled to so far have in place a hierarchy created by white people, that not only safeguards them from violence, but also offers them privileges not afforded to the black natives of these countries. Even as the minority in the local population, they still feel a sense of majority, because they are given control and access to resources and power to the functionality of the government. Most black people in Africa and the Caribbean tend to look to their black leaders and the general black population, to point fingers whenever the topics of corruption, dysfunction, poor government, and lack of access to services are discussed, in order to establish blame for their unperceived exploitation. Their lack of knowledge and naiveté about white oppression and manipulation often keep them in the dark, because they can't see the puppeteer pulling the strings of the puppets that are often selected to run their countries into the ground.

We are all brothers and sisters, and we're not that much different, except that the imperialists have subjected us to different customs from the time they separated us from our true culture, heritage, religious practices, and language in Africa. They kidnapped our forefathers, and forced them into slavery for the benefit of white privilege around the world, and we continue to allow them that access and privilege. Our marginalization may be different, but their end goal is to keep all black people subjugated worldwide, even on their own continent in Africa. Not one white racist police officer, in the history of racism, has ever taken the time to inquire about which country a black person is from while pulling them over, before acting maliciously racist toward them during a traffic stop or some other infraction. Racism is an endless chess game that white people want to continue to win, by confusing black people and other people of color about the tactics used to create division among them. The great divide among black people seems to be the advantage that white imperialism thrives on, but we can't seem to take off the blinders to see it for what it is. I try to cope daily with black people's struggles and difficulties to unite, and sometimes I feel like it's an endless battle. Still, I remain confident that one day, even the biggest sellout will have to reckon with the fact that he's totally blind to his own subjugation because the racist system has been able to shift the blame to the victims.

My grandparents, alone, were responsible for migrating my aging great-grandparents and all of their siblings from the South to the North. However, all the siblings helped one another financially for as long as they could, when they got to Boston, until each one could branch out on their own. Back then, the black family really supported one another. Boston, though one of the most racist cities in America at the time, seemed to have been full of opportunities for black folks who were looking for work, in a limited capacity and a certain sector of the job market, of course. A lot of the jobs were blue-collar positions that most white people, but especially the Irish, didn't want to do anymore, but black people found that they were much better than the menial cotton picking and busboy jobs in the Aouth, due to the Jim Crow restrictions that were in place. The Charlestown Navy Yard jobs were the cream of the crop at the time for many of the black people in Boston who were trying to carve a decent life for themselves, and many black men were able to find a job there.

In a way, it's easy for me to inter-relate the two struggles of my family and Candace's family, because it was about seeking better opportunities for both families, due to lack of opportunities created by oppressive systems. It seemed as if my grandparents' migration to the North was more about survival than anything. When you really think about it, most black people in this country are forced into survival mode, most of the time, which restricts their ability to just live. A lot of black people around the world have never truly lived life throughout their lifetime, because of the many obstacles they face in order to survive. Many of us are in constant survival mode, because we often have to resort to side hustles just to provide the basic necessities for ourselves and our family, in addition to constantly trying to avoid the pitfalls established by the racist system in society to destroy us, such as police brutality, drugs, crime and so many other elements that exist in the ghetto for the sole destruction of black people. Even myself, decades after the Jim Crow laws have been somewhat eradicated but still practiced in many ways, because they seem to have taken on a new form across America, I'm still in survival mode. I'm talking decades after the suffering of my great-grandparents, but I'm still feeling the lingering effects of slavery and Jim Crow in the North. While Bill Clinton and Biden's Mass incarceration legislation is the most famous modern day Jim Crow law that has ever been passed by liberal whites who call themselves friends of the black community, there are many other laws on the books to subjugate black people to this day, and police have the latitude to criminalize any black man at will, however and whenever it suits them. Resisting arrest or disorderly conduct are the two most common Jim Crow charges practiced by cops against black people in what I call modern day slavery. Not even body-cams can stop their practice of marginalizing and killing black people unjustly. The body-cams were supposed to offer relief, transparency, and peace of mind to black people, as it relates to interaction with cops, so the system could pacify black people, and unfortunately, too many of my people fell for the banana in the tailpipe. Even video footage of cops abusing and killing black people is not enough to convince grand juries across the nation to charge white cops who commit egregiously dangerous crimes against black people. Too often, the video footage they present to the public after a black person has been murdered by police is manipulated before its release. I have no idea what it would take to eradicate racism among police officers across the country, but body-cams is not the solution. I don't know when a racist cop might decide to take my life and decides to justify it by lying about me reaching for a gun, a lie that is prevalent in 95 percent of police shooting, and an excuse that is taught at the police academies across the country. I'm happy every time I make it back home safely and alive to my family, because these police officers are out here killing young black men indiscriminately, and most of the time, they get away with it.

I don't expect to receive any special treatment as a veteran who has served his country, because this country has always disrespected black veterans, but I do require some kind of courtesy for having risked my life in Iraq and Afghanistan to defend this country under the false pretenses used by this government for their invasion of other countries in the world. We have never fought a war to defend America. Every modern war that American veterans have fought in the last fifty years was an invasion by the US in other countries. Clearly, I know how to defend myself, and I intend to do just that in any situation where aggression against me is unwarranted. I'm a gun-carrying citizen who obeys all the laws of the land, but if some cop thinks he can violate my rights as a citizen because he's part of a sector of a Klan that carries badges and guns, it's just going to have to take 12 jurors to decide my fate, because I won't be the one going six feet under in a box, no matter who it is.

Since World War I, black soldiers have never been given the respect they deserve after risking their lives to "defend" the livelihood of Americans at home and abroad. I remember my great-grandfather telling us as children how he was mistreated and attacked by white people in his uniform, after returning home from Germany. Things would be no different after World War II for other black veterans who returned home, because white fragility feared an attack by the trained black soldiers, and decided to go on an offensive attack against these soldiers for no reason across the nation, but especially in the south, where racists refused to acknowledge the service and valor of returning black soldiers. To this day, black veterans are still disrespected by cops across the country. We have seen many incidents caught on body-cams where white cops have unjustly abused black veterans, and those cops usually go unpunished. This government has always seen its soldiers as expendable, but black soldiers especially, have never received the accolades and the respect they deserve. Even with the GI Bill, which was created to entice people to join the military during World War II, only the white soldiers were able to benefit from it after returning home from the war. Black soldiers were denied those benefits after returning home. The GI Bill helped create a white middle class when the white veterans returned home from the war, while the black soldiers were left hanging high and dry.

I knew all this history before I joined the military. I did my research prior to joining, so I could position myself to maximize the opportunity that I thought I would have as a marine. I never thought I would end up serving tours in Iraq and Afghanistan when I joined. They left the possibility of me serving tours overseas off the table, but as a soldier, I was trained and always ready. There's a history of black people in the military in this country that needs to be brought to the surface. While this racist government led black people in America to believe they weren't intellectually fit to serve in their army, the same racist government sought the assistance of Haitian soldiers during the Revolutionary War in 1779. It was the Haitian soldiers who helped the US win the Battle of

Savannah, while the government was trying to maintain a stronghold on slavery. The Haitians had demonstrated they were more than intellectually fit and capable of becoming soldiers and officers in their military when they helped defeat the British army. A few years later, the Haitian people would go on to defeat the mightiest army of them all, Napoleon's army, to gain their independence from France. Meanwhile, slavery lingered in America and black people were being lied to about their abilities, or lack thereof. Black people wouldn't be given the chance to join the Union Army until the Civil War in 1862, when Lincoln needed them, in order to defeat the Confederate Army. It's funny how a federal law was established in 1792 to prevent black people who were born on American soil from enlisting in the army, but the government somehow found a way to make an exception to allow for over 650 black Haitian soldiers to help them fight against the British. US history is full of conflicts and hypocrisies. I'm a history buff, so I research things that most people don't think about on a daily basis, especially as it relates to black history. I have always known that black history is not limited to what happened to black people in America. More importantly, I must point out that President Lincoln feared slave uprisings around the country after the Haitian Revolution, which is one of the main reasons he signed the Emancipation Proclamation. White people have never saved black people from anything, please don't get it confused. Lincoln needed the enslaved people to fight on behalf of the Union Army, or else they were going to revolt across the country.

Anyway, my goal was always to put myself in a position to earn a degree in engineering as a computer scientist, and I wanted to use the military as the vehicle to get that free college education. The US armed forces have never been fair to black people, and I didn't expect them to be fair to me. I have been disrespected by cops while in my Marine uniform, after getting pulled over by them. However, prior to rejoining civilian life, I was being disrespected in the military by men that I served with, subordinates, and higher-ranked officers. America's big selling point to the world, calling herself "The melting pot and the greatest country in the world" has always been an effective propaganda served to those people gullible enough to live on hope. A black man is just not safe in this country, no matter what he does to get out of harm's way, while a white man can carelessly murder dozens of people, and the police would still make his safety and humanity a priority.

POLICE, BRUTALITY AND THE BLACK COMMUNITY

Sometimes listening to my great grandparents, my grandparents and my parents' struggles, I question what has changed in America since their time, because I seem to be facing the same struggles in a different way. The narrative that America is the greatest country in the world is no longer propaganda around the world, because black athletes, musicians, and even the election of Obama, make it all believable and a reality. The illusion of freedom in America for all is openly sold and many people have bought into it. A lot of people have no idea that the police force emerged from the slave patrols centuries ago, but the tactics they've used to capture runaway slaves have never gone away, only now they victimize black people using those innovative tactics in a different way. Black people may not be running from the plantation, but most of us are constantly running from the police, even when we are just trying to avoid them. Black people may not be hunted down by dogs today, the same way they used to hunt down runaway slaves, but they are

still murdered the same way nonetheless, and hunting season for black men has never ended. I stand corrected. I have seen far too many videos of cops siccing their canines on subdued black men, for me to say that black people are no longer hunted down by dogs. I've had my share of situations where I was profiled for no reason by the cops, and they tried their best to criminalize me since I was a teenager. It would take all day for me to list the many different times and scenarios where cops have harassed and humiliated me publicly as a black man, without just cause. The laws on the books were created to protect white citizens but with the authority to violate the rights of black citizens indiscriminately. For the most part, even black cops who have committed their lives to the police force, sometimes have to learn and find out the hard way, that their rights aren't protected once they're out of uniform. And most of them aren't even aware of the double standard in place when it comes to conduct that is upheld for them and their white counterparts. While most white cops go unpunished for illegal infractions against black people, most black cops often face disciplinary action for illegal infractions against white people. At the end of the day, the system is there to protect white people in every aspect. My father taught me that at a young age.

I remember the days when my friends and I used to hang out on my front porch, you know, the house that my parents bought with their own money? We would be behind a closed gate, and these pigs would sometimes roll up on us for no reason, and try to step beyond the gate to harass us on my parents' property. They saw absolutely nothing wrong with violating our rights as young black people, because the system in place supported their behavior, and there was no repercussion to their destructive behavior against black people in our own community. In a way, when I think about it today as an adult, it appears as if the cops are rewarded for antagonizing the black community, because it helps to fill their established quota for arrests. Despite what they might say in the media, there is an arrest quota system in place for every black community established by all police departments across the country, which is why most cops feel empowered when they are violating the rights of black citizens. Thank goodness I had a dad who was not only huge, but also fearless, when it came to defending his family. My dad was quick to tell them to get the fuck off his property, whenever they were harassing us while he was around. My dad never feared the cops, as long as he knew he was within his rights to defend and protect his family. Those cowards were often too afraid to step up to my father, because he's a huge man.

What a lot of people, specifically black parents, don't understand, is that black children often don't have to look for trouble while walking around in their own neighborhood, but trouble always easily finds them whenever the cops are lurking. I'm not talking about being harassed for mischievous behavior, I'm talking about cops, for no reason, rolling up on black boys who are just walking home together, and they are labeled a gang by these race soldiers who often feel they have the right to violate their rights and criminalize them for no reason. That has happened to me personally as a youngster on numerous occasions while walking home with my friends. Patrol officers would harass us about walking the street for no reason, as if we have no right as black children to walk wherever the hell we wanted. However, many black parents are forced to believe that their children are in the wrong when they are harassed and wrongfully arrested by cops. We should not contribute to the criminalization of our own children. As a father, my job is to protect my children from harm, and I'm willing to do everything in my power to make sure they are safe at all times. The police are not an ally to the black community, and we should never become an ally to them against our own children. Still, the problem isn't so much that they get away with their bad behavior, but the fact that a lot of black parents are failing to bring their children to the local police stations to file complaints against these officers for harassment. My parents were always good with filing complaints on our behalf. They would write down an officer's name and badge number in a minute, and drive us down to the police station on Blue Hill Avenue to file a complaint for harassment. That's how they protected me and my siblings, and the cops were very familiar with them, and understood that my parents didn't play. The only problem, though, was my parents were probably the few people on our street who understood filing the complaints against these harassing officers was part of the paper trail needed to discipline these officers, whenever they overreacted during an infraction in the community. The entire neighborhood needed to understand that, because these racist assholes antagonized the entire black community. Even though my parents understood that most of these complaints went in the trash, they always made it clear to the sergeant in charge that they wanted copies of their complaints and kept copies of every complaint filed for their own records.

My parents knew that the police would never monitor bad police behavior, so it's up to the black community to keep records of their complaints, to hold them accountable. More black people need to learn to take the time to go to the police station to file these complaints, so that they can protect their children and their community. That would help to curb the bad behavior of some of these race soldiers who grew up in the suburbs but want to become cops in the urban black communities, without first learning and understanding the culture of the communities they sign up to work for. To be honest, I believe that most of them are in the black community to serve white supremacy, which is why the problem of police harassment persists to this day. The system doesn't want to correct police corruption. The Fraternal Order of Police is the most corrupt institution in America, and it's always been. This country has no right to tell anybody anything about human rights violations, because black people's rights are violated daily, and they haven't done a damn thing to change that.

Unfortunately, police reform will be a daunting task, because every police officer has been trained in systemic corruption, and bias is often implanted in their minds against black and brown people from the time they enroll at the police academy, to the time they work their way up the ranks of captain. The chain of command is corrupt from the source. A corrupt captain can never properly train a decent officer. Their blue code of silence is in place to make sure there's never such a thing as honest officers. Good cops aren't created, because good cops have to rely on bad cops for training, and as backup when they are dispatched to violent situations. It's a merry-go-round of corruption that will never cease. The blue wall of silence has allowed corruption to thrive in police departments across the country. They are all corrupted from the top down, even the ones who joined the force without prejudice. Senior officers usually pass down their corrupted tactics to all the rookie officers, to teach them the dirty ways to protect themselves against prosecution. Qualified immunity also doesn't help to curtail corruption. It's unfathomable to me that teachers, across the country, aren't allowed to carry guns, or even touch violent students in their classrooms, but cops can kill those same students outside of a classroom, sometimes without just cause, and still be protected through qualified immunity. Any teacher who dares put his or her hand on a student acting violently toward them in the classroom would get crucified for being aggressive toward such a violent student and would face termination, but cops can kill those same students in the street, without facing prosecution for their aggression toward a child. The problem starts with qualified immunity, and it can end with qualified immunity. Those police officers need to be held personally accountable every time they unjustly take someone's life, which is about 99% of the time in the black neighborhoods they patrol across America daily.

As I got older, I started to realize the way that the black community is policed by officers is no coincidence. First, the requirement to become a police officer in most major cities around the country is just a high school diploma, and to be 21 years of age. That's very basic, because even the biggest underachiever who manages to graduate from high school can easily be empowered to carry a gun and a badge to wreak havoc on a community. Second, the training that most police officers receive is not even suitable for the amount of mental preparation, poise, and psychological strength required. No 21 year-old can be trained within a three to six-month period to learn how to deal with the average criminal and potential killers. That's impossible, and learning on the job adds to the chaos and the mounting excessive force complaints that are filed annually by civilians. No training is rigorous enough for new police officers that only last 12-24 weeks, which can benefit the public at large, but especially black people, that most of these officers have never routinely encountered in their lives, and are often foreign to their culture.

Thousands of black men are sitting in prison because of coercion, false confessions, fear of a black man, and false arrests by police. No group of people in any other profession on earth has been allowed to lie like police officers. Perhaps, the politicians might have one up on them, but most of them are also involved in passing legislation that has to be carried out by their lying subordinate police officers who protect them at all costs. Most politicians are pro-law enforcement. Even when police officers are caught lying, there's often no consequences for their deception, because their lying superiors also rose through the ranks lying about their mischievous behavior on the job. Most police officers learn their lying tactics at the academy, and most are loyal to their oath to the blue wall of silence. There's no reforming this dishonorable and unprincipled organization in any way. That institution needs to be completely demolished, in order to bring integrity to police work. Then again, the police institution was never founded on integrity. It's the most corrupt culture around the world behind politicians. However, America leads the charge in police corruption, which is why it also leads the world in incarcerated people. There's no such thing as the few spoiling the bunch, because it's the bunch spoiling the few. Most cops are liars and corrupt, and the few good cops are always silenced with threats when the bunch is acting in a corrupted way. No integrity or high standard is required from police officers, even though that's what all police departments pride themselves on. Prosecutors often forgo real evidence while working in cahoots with police to corroborate their lies, so those prosecutors can build their careers as politicians or private practice criminal attorneys after serving publicly as prosecutors. They get to experience and understand both sides of the law, which makes them better defense attorneys. The more conviction they're able to get, the quicker their public careers advance. Being tough on crime is a selling point for all prosecutors across the country, because they can use their conviction rate to promote their political careers and private practices after leaving their public post. Rudy Giuliani prosecuted the toughest mobsters in New York, before branching off into politics, and then disgracing himself as the liar that he had always been under the Trump administration.

There's a domino effect to police corruption, which makes prosecutors and judges complicit. Everything about corruption in the police department is systemic because police practices require cops to always work as a gang or a unit that believes they are untouchable, in order to instill fear and take control over situations where they are afraid themselves. They have to do everything in their power to maintain their reputation as the most powerful entity around the world. There's actually no limit to the power of a police officer, unless he's caught red-handed committing an illegal act. However, their power is mostly exercised in certain demographics and against marginalized groups of people they know are powerless. Black and brown people are the only people who have allowed the police to exert so much power over them for so long, without actually revolting against them. At some point, the minority communities are going to have to rise and start fighting back. Bullying people around has its limits. There are far more people than police officers anywhere in America, and the way the gun laws are written here, it's a matter of time before everyone is armed and the people should be able to outgun the police with no problem. These are not my observations. It's the absolute truth. Texas and Georgia have gone back to a cowboy state where a permit is no longer required to carry a gun. That's a civil war waiting to happen. Once everyone becomes armed, (hopefully black people are not late to that party) the police will start acting accordingly. These so-called public servants are owned by the elites, and their job is to reinforce a systemic type of slavery that has been in place in this country for centuries, which was established to benefit slave owners at the inception of this country. The corroboration of racist prosecutors, judges, along with police officers, makes it difficult to bring honesty and integrity into the American justice system. The old racists shed their white robes and hoods for police badges, black robes, and law degrees. The perfect word to describe injustice in America is racism. The discrepancy in which Judges hand out sentences to black and white people who commit the same crimes is a travesty to justice itself. Some of these judges need to be under a jail cell for being complicit to injustice, while living in a country that boasts freedom and equality for all. America has never been about freedom and equality for all. Even as Thomas Jefferson wrote in his constitution "All men are created equal," he still held slaves, and was raping quite a few of them without prejudice, as one of the racist founding fathers of this country. The hypocrisy in American history and society is ludicrous.

BLACK PEOPLE'S POSITION IN THE WORLD.

It would take a lifetime to explain the undertakings of white supremacy against the most vulnerable group of people in this world, which is people of African descent. Black people worldwide are vulnerable, because the leaders of African nations have never prioritized Africa's military might in the world, technology, scientific development, and overall infrastructure. The entire continent of Africa is bullied and exploited, because most African nations lack the firepower, technology, military training, and the arsenal to destroy their European and American adversaries. Still, Africa possesses the most natural resources and wealth to control the entire world. In essence, people of African descent all over the world are vulnerable to white supremacy, because they have nowhere to run for protection. South Africa was strengthened militarily, because of apartheid. White people ran South Africa for years, so they were allies of these white imperialists in the West. As a former Marine, I understand the confidence that the United States government has in its armed forces. We are responsible for training most of the military juntas across Africa, and use them at will, whenever we want to dispose of a leader in Africa that America and its racist allies don't like. This division among African leaders was solidified when the Europeans decided to meet in Berlin in 1884 to carve up Africa for their own benefit and interests. Instead of focusing on uniting the entire continent of Africa, individual puppet leaders who are placed in power by the West, are coerced into becoming traitors against their own brothers and sisters, thus, making it easier for the Europeans and Americans to strengthen their exploitative tactics against Africa. Black people will never be respected anywhere in the world, until the African continent is strengthened militarily, and offers professional and educated people of African descent the option to return to the motherland to help assist with development in all areas. Until then, black people in the diaspora will do everything in their power to adjust to their marginalization, subjugation, exploitation and oppression in the West, because most of them don't see Africa as a better option than white supremacy and the racism they have experienced.

In America alone, there are millions of experienced of black soldiers and higher ranked officers who can help Africa develop militarily, but those African puppets masquerading as leaders, don't them as an option. Africa has put no effort in recruiting black professionals to come back to Africa to help develop the continent. Instead, they go to the Chinese and other governments in the West, where they can secure loans that can be paid to those leaders directly, while risking losing the natural resources to China and the West, because those loans are backed by African natural resources the rest of the world needs. Africa should not depend on the Chinese or Europeans for development, when there are so many professional people of African descent in every corner of the world. Africa should be the first option for all black professionals, but that is not the case, because African leaders are more concerned about lining up their personal pockets than making sure Africans earn descent and livable wages, have proper sanitation and healthcare, access to free education, and so many other variables that can make Africa a powerhouse in the world. Until all that happens, the African diaspora will continue to bend backwards to make every adjustment necessary to survive within the construct of white supremacy and white imperialism. These people in the West always unite when it's time to exploit Africa, because they understand their strength in numbers. However, we can't get enough African leaders to come together to discuss the future of Africa, without everyone looking for their own opportunity, self-interest and the interests of their family and friends, to exploit their own people. We're basically our own worse enemy...

TO BE
CONTINUED IN
PART 2...

Made in the USA
Middletown, DE
08 October 2023